INTO THE
FUTURE

Other Books of Frank O'Loughlin

Does sin matter?

Gathering the People of God

New wineskins

The future of the sacrament of Penance

THE CATHOLIC CHURCH

INTO THE
FUTURE

FRANK O'LOUGHLIN

COVENTRY
PRESS

Published in Australia by
Coventry Press
33 Scoresby Road
Bayswater VIC 3153

ISBN 9781922589521

Copyright © Frank O'Loughlin 2024

All rights reserved. Other than for the purposes and subject to the conditions prescribed under the *Copyright Act*, no part of this publication may be reproduced, stored in a retrieval system, or transmitted in any form or by any means, electronic, mechanical, photocopying, recording or otherwise, without the prior permission of the publisher.

Scripture quotations are from the *New Jerusalem Bible*, copyright © 1985, by Darton, Longman & Todd, Ltd. and Doubleday, a division of Random House, Inc. Reprinted by Permission.

Catalogue-in-Publication entry is available from the National Library of Australia
http://catalogue.nla.gov.au

Cover design by Ian James – www.jgd.com.au
Text design by Coventry Press
Set in EB Garamond

Printed in Australia

Contents

Foreword 6

Part 1   Moving into the future 9

Chapter One: A new culture, a new context 11
Chapter Two: Called into the future 19
Chapter Three: Moving into the future 28
Chapter Four: What is to be left behind? 45
Chapter Five: What will the future hold? 65

Part 2   What do we take with us into the future? 75

Introduction 77
Chapter Six: Faithful to the teaching of the Apostles 80
Chapter Seven: Faithful to the Fellowship 96
Chapter Eight: Faithful to the Breaking of the Bread . 107
Chapter Nine: Faithful to Prayer 121

Conclusion 130
Appendix: A Model for the Future 132

FOREWORD

Human beings live their lives in the present but in doing so they emerge out of their past and move into their future. What the future will be may be presumed, imagined and planned for but it is not known. This is a pattern of human life that is not optional; it is built into the nature of being a human being. This movement into the future is sometimes plain sailing and, at other times, occurs in rough waters. It is always tied to changing historical events and circumstances, to differing social and cultural conditions and to the decisions of those people whose positions affect the lives of others in major and minor ways.

In its long history, the Church has had to keep moving into the future, sometimes in organised and sometimes in disorganised ways; sometimes it wanted to move ahead and at other times it did not. And such movements into the future occurred at different times and in different places; sometimes they affected the whole Church and at other times only certain parts of the Church. Dealing with the change – which is part of such movement into the future – is not an option but the way it is dealt with is. It has been dealt with differently at different times and in different places.

In reaction to new challenges, the Church can be tempted to withdraw into itself and try to ignore what is going on in the world around it. However, the Catholic tradition insists that the Church is not a sect that seeks self-sufficiency and separation from the world; but rather it is the People of God made up of human beings living among other human beings. The Church is made up of human beings who have been invited into a deeper discovery of God in Jesus Christ who gave his life not just for them but for all. Pope Francis constantly calls the Church to go beyond itself and be oriented to humankind which it is called to serve, that is to be a Church that does not close up within itself but goes out of itself.

Fear is the enemy of change and of the future. Fear makes human beings shrink into themselves and diminish. The same awaits the Church if it decides to let fear have its way as we move into the future.

The Church's ultimate strength is in God who is utterly faithful; his faithful love knows no end as we sing at the Easter Vigil (Psalm 117(118): 1-4). God's fidelity is the ultimate source of our confidence as we journey into the future. There are those who fear that the Church is threatened with death in these times. And we do indeed live in times that call for a radical reappraisal of the Church's ways. A reappraisal that requires a re-immersion in the gospel of Jesus Christ.

The People of God, the Church, in its strength and its weakness, its holiness and its sinfulness, is constantly accompanied through all of its history by the God whose fidelity is unending. He has constantly opened a way ahead before his people. His people, of course, must respond by entering onto the way he opens up before them.

Part 1
Moving into the future

Chapter One

A NEW CULTURE, A NEW CONTEXT

A secularising culture

A French theologian who visited Australia a few years back made the comment that he felt that the Church in Australia was still afraid of the secular and pluralist society of which it was part. I find that observation a useful starting point for a book entitled *Into the Future*. The Church in France has been living with a secular and pluralist culture for a long time and has moved towards coming to grips with it, while also experiencing the considerable disagreement and conflict which arise whenever and wherever the Church finds itself in a new cultural situation.

The Church in Australia has not been living within the secular society for as long as the Church in France, but it is now very clear that Australian society is thoroughly secular and will remain so into the future. It is crucial that this be taken into account in considering the Church's future. This secular context is, in the commonly used phrase, the 'new normal'! And that has been the case for quite some time.

In speaking of a secular society, I mean that the workings of such a society and its culture are in principle secular, that is it does not have any inherent reference to God or to the transcendent in its social, cultural and political settings. Inherently, it functions as if there is no God. Explicit and serious reference to God has been formally excised from most Western societies and their cultures. Secularity is part of the mindset of such cultures. A long process covering several centuries lies behind the formation of secular societies and their removal of the religious dimension of human life.

As a result of this established secularity, such societies are in practice not simply secular but secularising, that is they have an inbuilt tendency to form secular attitudes in their members. The inherent power of societies to shape their members in their own image is at work in secular societies, just as it was at work in the religious societies of the past with their tendency to shape their members religiously. These tendencies are strong social forces and are an effective means of shaping the taken-for-granted attitudes in the members of any society.

But just as religious societies do not always succeed in making all their members religious, so secular societies do not always succeed in making all their members secular. There are always those – both groups and individuals – who are able to stand back from the prevailing social attitudes and take a different stand which is not necessarily one of opposition to the society, but can be insightfully critical of the society's unexplored presumptions and of the gaps in its thinking. Having secular attitudes is not of itself a sign of being intelligent – as some would have it – but can simply be an instance of going along with the crowd.

There are, of course, religious people in secular societies; they may even be more numerous than is commonly acknowledged. The significant point of difference in the contemporary secular society to earlier societies is the fact that faith in God is no longer seen as part of the social structure or ethos in secularising societies. Secular attitudes have been established in the institutions of such societies, and so they influence their laws, their popular customs and their ethical attitudes. Belief in God – that was once largely taken for granted – is no longer an element in such a society's presumed understanding of the world.

Religiousness has become an option for individuals within secularised societies. Religiousness is one possible option for people; it is one option among many other possible options available in a pluralist society for an understanding of life and the world.[1]

Referring again to the above comment about fear of the secular society in the Australian Church, an alternative response to the Church's living in a secular society is to see the Church as a unique resource for the secular society – an enriching resource and a positively critical resource based in the gospel of Jesus Christ and a long experience of the doings of human beings. Such a Christian response to the secular requires mutual respect and sincere dialogue between them.

Living in a secular society is a relatively new experience for the Church and calls for a new presentation of the gospel of Jesus Christ which is to be looked forward to and not feared. It opens up a new and creative future for the gospel and the Church. Secular societies are to be taken seriously but not to be feared. Like all things human, they have their limitations and inadequacies. It is looking backwards which is to be feared!

Religion and society

In this section, I would like to develop further the differences between the secular societies of the present and the religious societies of the past. In earlier centuries, religiousness was tightly woven into the structures of societies and that social arrangement prevailed for a very long time. Not to be Christian was not a realistic option in Medieval and Early Modern European society; it was

---

[1] For a thorough development of this idea see: Charles Taylor, 'Shapes of Faith Today', in Charles Taylor, Jose Casanova, George F McLean, Joao J. Vila-Cha (eds), *Renewing the Church in a Secular Age*. Washington: The Council for Research in Values and Philosophy, 2016, 269 – 281; and Hans Joas, *Faith as an Option. Possible Futures for Christianity*. Stanford, California: Stanford University Press, 2014.

simply a dimension of being European. It was taken for granted. Those societies functioned in the same manner as strictly Islamic societies function today. Until the last couple of centuries, western societies were formally, explicitly and legally Christian; as societies, they explicitly professed Christianity. Christianity was woven into their functioning. This is obviously no longer the case!

Religiousness in contemporary Western societies tends to pluralistic: it is made up of different religious traditions all of which are in principle of equal social status. There are many and varied religious and spiritual traditions in such societies, none of which is given official social and political standing in their structures. Consequently, in such a situation, religiousness is seen as a matter left up to the choice of each individual.

As Christian believers, we have an inheritance from a culturally religious past. We have inherited a Christianity which until the late nineteenth century shaped public and private life. It determined the organisation of space in cities and villages (around the parish church), the way the year was organised (the feasts and seasons), the way the world was perceived (for example, it all began with Adam and Eve). It shaped family relationships. It formed the social symbols of identity (such as the coalescence of human initiation and Christian initiation in baptism and confirmation). In such cultures, the religious dimension of life was quite unavoidable and was part of people's social and cultural identity.

Such a union of society and religion was not only true of European countries and their offshoots, but the same social and political structural pattern was in place – and in some instances still is in place – wherever religion and society are inherently interlaced. This is the case in strictly Islamic societies but also in countries where Hinduism or Buddhism are virtually established religions.

Plurality

Above, I have been emphasising the secular character of our society because that is the 'established' attitude in our society. There is another important characteristic of contemporary secular societies and that is that they are pluralistic, as was mentioned above. Because the secular society steps back from any direct religious stance, it also generates a plurality of approaches to life and the world – a plurality of religious and non-religious approaches and attitudes. As a result, there is in such societies a wide range of differing attitudes to the meaning of human life and of the world. People may explicitly adopt one or other of such options explicitly or they may simply fall in with one or other of these approaches by a sort of osmosis without any significant consideration or commitment.

One of the characteristics of secular societies is the rise of a strong desire to find a spirituality that takes more account of people's overall humanity than does the ethos of the secular society. There is probably a strong thread in this desire to fill the gap left by the disappearance of religion from the lives of so many people.

In line with this desire for spirituality, we see the arrival of many forms of Eastern religions in Western societies. And we also see many newly coined forms of spirituality, some of which are religious in character and others which are not. Many of these are nature-based and some call upon pagan religious forms of the ancient Western civilisations.

We are also witnessing what has been called 'the return of religion'.[2] There was once the presumption – accompanying talk of secularisation – that it would bring about the end of religion. As time has gone on this has not proved to be true. Secularisation seems to be dominant in many Western countries but it has not brought about the end of religion and its very rise has brought about religious reactions to it. We have seen the rise of fundamentalisms in all the major religions which reject the secular society and seek to replace it.

---

[2] See for instance, Graham Ward and Michael Hoelzl (eds), *The New visibility of Religion*. London, UK & NY: Continuum, 2008.

Whatever the mix of dynamics at work in secular societies, secular attitudes remain very determinative of the shape and ethos of such societies.

The pluralism present in contemporary societies changes the ancient conception of religion as that which binds a society together,[3] which fact opens up one of the big questions for secular societies: what does in fact hold them together?

Into the future

As we move into the future, the context within which faith in Christ will be lived out in Western cultures will be secular and pluralist. As suggested above, this is 'the new normal'.

Given this changed situation, it is crucial that we cease clinging to our past and get over grieving for it. As is the case in any form of grief, we have to move on into the new situation and not remain trapped in our grief, or lost in nostalgia for the past. We can continue to honour and love the past without letting ourselves be enclosed by it. As Christian believers, we continue to honour and appreciate our past while also being ready to move into a different future. Every period of history is shaped by particular circumstances, events and attitudes. No era can be considered as an absolute or a 'golden age' which needs to be re-established.

The history of the Christian Tradition illustrates that this is the way in which that tradition has progressed: its various stages have been launching pads into the future, even amidst accompanying conflicts. As in an earlier book, I would like to quote a saying attributed to Pablo Picasso which is that tradition is not wearing your grandfather's hat but having a child. Tradition is not just repeating or imitating the past; it is a handing on into the future. And that future cannot be presupposed or predetermined. In

---

[3] The word 'religion' is derived from the Latin *religare* which means 'to bind together'.

having a child, the child has a radical rootedness in those who have gone before them but that child's future is open-ended and not predetermined. So it is with tradition in the Church. To acknowledge this is especially important in a time of radical transition like our own.

Seeing the secular society as the current and future context in which the Christian faith is to be lived means that we have to cease expecting that specifically Christian attitudes will necessarily be prevalent in our society. Other attitudes to social, cultural, political and moral issues will be forthcoming and will, at times, be preferred by a majority of people in the overall society.

Similarly, we need to cease being surprised that young people do not automatically take up the faith in which they have been raised. The culture in which they live will have its influence on them. And in handing on the faith, that culture has to be taken into account. People are no longer able to absorb a religious culture from their surrounds because their surrounds are no longer religious. People will have to come to faith in the gospel of Christ by different means than was the case in the past.

As said above, every society and its culture is a powerful influence on the shaping of the identity of its members. We need to take into account that prevailing cultures penetrate their members and tend to create them in their own image. And given that Christians are called to belong to their society and not withdraw from it, they will be subject to the same powerful social and cultural influences as their fellow citizens. We can see this influence at work in the generations belonging to the Church today in their varying degrees of adherence to and practice of the faith.

The faith has always been lived within a culture. From its deeply Jewish origins, the Christian faith has been lived within the culture of its time and place. From New Testament times on, it has had to learn to transition out of one culture into another. This is a complex process and it is witnessed to as early as the New Testament writings themselves. Today, we have to learn to live in the given secularising culture as the context in which we are called to be believers.

Into the Future

Believers today need to live their faith and understand it within the secular and pluralist culture of which they are part. Talk of Faith and Culture has been a theme in discussions about 'mission countries' for more than a century, but it is no less an issue for countries which were once formally Christian but which are now secular and pluralist. A faith once nurtured and developed in a religious culture will today find itself buffeted by the strong winds of contemporary culture, it will be questioned rather than presumed, and will be regarded by some as obsolete. This transition from one culture to another requires serious discernment which we will discuss as this book proceeds.

When everyone in a society believes the same thing, that belief tends to be seen as a fact of life rather than a belief. This tendency had a christianising effect in earlier centuries when Christianity was seen as part of the social make-up. At that time, Christianity was the common sense of the time. In secular societies, a secular attitude becomes the common sense of the time. Secular attitudes tend to be considered as facts rather than as a particular and limited approach to life and reality.

Secular attitudes are not the only acceptable approach to human life and the reality of the world, but a secularising culture can tend to make it seem so. This calls on Christian believers to present and nourish a different approach by entering into dialogue with the mentality of the secularising society; a dialogue which needs to be open and can be mutually enriching and positively critical.

Chapter Two

CALLED INTO THE FUTURE

Seeking to understand the situation of the Church in an age of transition such as is ours, we can find an enlightening thread running through the whole biblical tradition which we can tap in to. That thread consists in a constant call to the People of God to move on into a future that God holds out to them.

Past events and the present

In order to appreciate the importance of this thread of tradition, we need to realise that the history of God's dealings with his people recounted in the Scriptures is not just a recounting of events that belong to the past. Those events are not locked in the past; rather, they are events that are symbolic for the People of God. In these events, we can catch reflections of the God with whom we are in relationship in our present moment of time. These past events are revealing of the God we are relating to now. They provide a means of discovering in our present time inspired pathways into the future.

These revealing events are to be interpreted within the limits of the stage of development and circumstances of the time in which they occurred. God's revealing of himself in human history is limited by the understanding and culture of those involved in that particular relationship with God at that time of history. Throughout biblical history there is a process of gradual refinement of the understanding of God and, in that light, of the meaning of human existence.

The *patterns* of God's approach to his people in the past give us insight into God and God's ways with human beings. So the God who called Israel out of slavery in Egypt is the God who is always seeking to set people free and to lead them into a new future. The events of the past recounted in the Scriptures are signs which we are called to ponder and interpret in order to discover God's ever present activity among his People and his constant presence and influence in his world.

At the heart of the Scriptures, there are core events by means of which the People of God began to know the true God and to discover the nature of God's call to them. These events display patterns to be remembered at every stage of the journey of God's People through history in order that they might discover their way ahead. These events were handed down in tradition and were written into the Scriptures so that the People of God might discover God again in new times and in new circumstances.

The scriptural narratives are written without much concern for the details of the past but with a deep concern for God's presence and action not only in the past but in the present and the future. Their purpose is to act as the means of revealing the presence of God and the continuing ways in which God is at work throughout the history of his People and in the midst of humankind. Let us now look at some of those events.

The call of Abraham

If we go back to the accounts of the call and life of Abraham in the Book of Genesis (chapter 12 to chapter 22), we find that he is called to leave his father's house and go to a land which God would show him:

> "The Lord said to Abraham, 'Leave your country, your kindred and your father's house for a country that I will show you; and I shall make you into a great nation, I shall

bless you and make your name famous; you are to be a blessing!'" (Genesis 12:1-3).

Abraham is called away from all that has been his life to that point. He is called to leave his father, his home and kin and move into a future about which God's call is rather vague: he is called into a land that God 'would show him'! He has to leave his past behind; he has to set out on the journey into which he is called, without any concrete, determined destination. Even the name his father gave him, Abram, is changed to Abraham. He has to make a journey of faith! Abraham is traditionally called 'our father in faith' because of the act of faith and trust which God had evoked in him. Abraham sets a pattern for all believers to come.

In leaving his father's house, Abraham is breaking with the cultural expectations of his people and his time. He is not doing what is expected of a son within his culture. What he does creates a break within the culture of his time. While being within that culture and bearing it within him, he creates a break with it from which something new emerges. We could say that the tradition of which he is part, produces a new offshoot by means of the breach he creates by leaving his father's house, thereby setting a new course. This also involves his leaving behind the gods of his father and his kin to begin to know the One who will be called – among other names – 'the God of Abraham'. Just as this God changed his name, so Abraham will give his name to this God, who will thereby be definitively associated with Abraham.

In this call, God does not take away Abraham's freedom. Abraham has to work through the issues which factually arise as he sets out on this long journey. In all his ups and downs, what is significant is that God keeps opening a way before him, a way to move on into the promised future.

The Exodus

In the central event of Israel's history – the Exodus – Israel is called out of slavery in Egypt into a new future in a land of its own. But this involved a long journey through a desert during which they encountered obstacles that impeded their onward journey and made the past seem attractive: in their frustration, they referred to their enslaved past as the 'fleshpots' of Egypt (Exodus 16:3).

The resolution of these obstacles are recounted in wondrous and epic form in the scriptural narratives. Yet each of them is resolved in terms of faith in the God who keeps opening a way before his people. The crossing of the Red Sea is epically recounted as the great instance of God's opening a way before them, creating an exit out of a situation which seemed to spell doom for them as they were caught between the waters of the Red Sea and the oncoming Egyptian army.

But this crossing of the sea was but a step along the way; it was not a resolution of all the difficulties that would arise. There was still a journey to be done. The actual Exodus through the Red Sea was simply a highly significant instance of God's opening of a way before his People. They are constantly being called ahead, despite their recurrent fear and hesitancy regarding the way ahead into which God was calling them.

And the way ahead was never purely an action of God, excluding them from participation and necessary action in what occurred. It was always a call and an enabling which had to be accepted and put into action in their own forward movement. It was always part of a covenant, of a relationship between God and themselves, in which each had their part to play.

The Exile

In the sixth century before Christ, Israel was conquered by the Assyrians and a significant part of the people was taken into captivity in Babylon where they remained in exile for some decades. This was traumatic not just for those taken captive but for the whole of Israel. This was so because, in the course of the Assyrian conquest, their temple was destroyed, their priesthood was scattered and ceased to function, and, most significantly, they lost possession of the land that the Lord had given them at the end of the Exodus, their Promised Land.

Their question at the time of the Exile was – had God deserted them? Were they no longer God's chosen people? The land which was the effective sign of the Exodus and so of their being God's chosen people was now no longer theirs! The possession of the land was indeed the end product and the fruit of the Exodus. They entered into a radical and soul-searching crisis!

After some decades, their captors, the Assyrians, were themselves conquered by the Persians whose leader set the Israelites free to return to their own land. This new start for Israel was enabled by the pagan king of the Persians, Cyrus, in whom they perceived an instrument of God, of God opening a way before them. They were set free and enabled return to their own land.

Again, a way was opened up before them. Yet again, all their problems were not solved for them but they had a new start. Their expectations were not fulfilled as they had thought they would be but a way into the future was given to them.

Jesus the Messiah

We can see the same pattern of God's opening a way before his people in the life, death and resurrection of Jesus in a much more radical and universal sense.

Jesus is caught in the grip of those who seek his death and they do indeed kill him. Those immediately involved in the death of Jesus – Pontius Pilate, the religious leaders, the fickle mob, Judas Iscariot – are representatives of forces that are always at work among human beings. Those involved in Jesus' death are representatives of the misuse of power and of human self-centredness which have distorted human life in the past and continue to do so in the present. This self-centredness and misuse of power has the capacity to bring death and diminishment to human beings. It was the misuse of such power that killed Jesus, as it has killed so many others before and after him.

The response of the Father to Jesus' death is to raise him out of death, that is the Father opened a way through death before him; he opened a way through death into life beyond both death and human evil. This was not what any of the protagonists involved in his death expected, nor did his own disciples expect it.

The human attitudes and actions of those who brought about the death of Jesus are still at work among human beings in our time as they have been in all times. But a way ahead out of them has been forged into a new and unexpected future beyond the power of any of those ever-present human forces that were at work in Jesus' death. He was subject to and eventually victorious over the forces which continue to bring about human suffering and death.

Following his death, the disillusioned disciples of Jesus were confronted by his living presence which they came to understand and express by reference to what God had done in the past. The discovery that the life, death and resurrection of Jesus was actually "according to the Scriptures" was made by reference to many texts of the Old Testament.

The core reference was to the Exodus which Israel celebrated at every Passover. And so Jesus' death and resurrection was called the Paschal Mystery, that is the Mystery of Jesus' Exodus or Passover. The new Exodus had occurred in his death and resurrection; a new way ahead was opened up through death, and despite the power of those human sinful attitudes which brought about his death. This opens the way ahead for all humankind.

The resurrection brought the first disciples into a changed situation; it involved his disciples in a new relationship with Jesus. It required a transition from the discipleship to which they had been accustomed during his earthly life to a discipleship which involved contact and communion with him as risen. They had to move out of what they were used to into a new future.

That earlier relationship is reflected in the narratives of the gospels which present a situation where the disciples could see and touch Jesus and hear his actual words; they could mix with him as they could with other people. This relationship had to be left behind and they had to feel their way towards relating to him without seeing, touching and hearing and enter into those things which gave them access to him as risen Lord. What those things are is summarily mentioned in the Acts of the Apostles (2:42): the handing down of what Jesus had said and done (the teaching of the apostles), the believing community (the fellowship), the Eucharist (the breaking of the bread) and prayer. It is those four things to which those first Christians were called to be faithful, and to which all Christians are called to be faithful, that will structure the second part of this book.

The New Testament church

The same pattern of a call into the future is present in the earliest decades of Christianity. In those early years, there was a transition of the initial group of disciples out of the world and religion of Judaism into the pagan world of the Graeco-Roman Empire, in which Christianity would eventually spread its wings.

Among those early believers in Christ, there were those who held that Christianity needed to remain within the confines of Judaism and thought that to become a Christian, one had first to become Jewish. In a way, this was understandable enough, as Jesus had lived his life within Judaism both religiously and culturally and so, they thought, should his followers.

But very quickly, Peter in the house of Cornelius (Acts 10:1-48) and then especially Paul took to heart that Jesus the Christ was for all humankind and that he and his kingdom were to be proclaimed to all the nations. This approach was affirmed by a gathering of the Christian leaders in Jerusalem which is reported in the Acts of the Apostles 15:1-34. This gathering has sometimes been called the 'Council of Jerusalem', by reference to the calling of later Ecumenical Councils in order to resolve difficulties in the life of the Church.

For some Christians, this transition beyond Judaism was not acceptable and they continued to believe that Christianity had to remain within the confines of Judaism. Some of these Christians eventually separated themselves from the communion of the Churches.

We see again in this conflict the pattern of a call to move into the future. It is clearly presented as a call in the above mentioned narrative of Peter in the house of Cornelius, as it is in the call of the risen Christ to Paul and then in Paul's subsequent writings.

This pattern of movement into the future is a constant characteristic of the biblical faith and of the living tradition of the Church.

The present

Pondering the events of the Old and New Testaments in which God's dealings with his people are recounted, we can see patterns by means of which we can discern the presence and invitation of the living God who has been, is now, and will always be at work among his people.

In the situation in which we find ourselves today, which we have called the new normal of the secularising society, a way ahead will be given to us, a movement out of and beyond the problems which seem to encircle us, a movement into a *new* future. As has been the case in the past, the way ahead will not be quite what we expect. It will require adjustments to our expectations, our thinking and our way of life and it will not be without its problems.

Is it not significant that a journey is so prominent a part of the above scriptural events? It is there in the Abraham story and in the

Exodus as it is in the Exile and return from exile. It is there in the death and resurrection of Jesus which we call the Passover Mystery, that is the Mystery of Jesus' journey through his life and his death to the Father and a new life.

Journey is essentially about going somewhere, about moving ahead, about a future into which those on the journey are moving. Vatican II calls the People of God the Pilgrim People of God, that is the People of God who are on a journey, a journey which is a constant part of its life as it is also a part of all human life.

In his attitudes, words and symbolic actions, Pope Francis is a sign of this call into the future. Pope Francis keeps reading the situation in which the Church finds itself today; he does not so much have an agenda to implement, but rather seeks to respond to the concrete situations in which the Church finds itself. This can mean that he disappoints people who are both to the right and to the left of him whose purpose is to implement an agenda.[4]

The call to move into the future requires attentive listening, response and action. It involves what Psalm 5, verse 4 describes as 'watching and waiting'. The call continues and seeks to arouse response from contemporary believers. The response can be fragile and bedevilled by fear and a lack of willingness to move beyond the situation in which we find comfort and security. And the call can also be refused.

The hesitancy and even the refusal to move on has been present in the moments of the history of God's people presented above. Nonetheless, the movement into the future has always been and remains the way into which God calls his People, a call the faithful God never gives up on.

---

[4] See Austen Ivereigh, 'Hearing the Spirit in the Assembly of the People: Pope Francis' vision of Synodality', in (ed.) Massimo Borghesi, *Da Bergoglio a Francesco. Un pontificato nella storia*. Roma: Edizioni Studium, 2022, 98-112.

Chapter Three
MOVING INTO THE FUTURE

Being in transition

Whenever there is a significant transition into the future there are things which have to be left behind.

We saw in the last chapter that this was so for Abraham, as it was for Israel in the Exodus and the Exile, as it was in the death and resurrection of the Lord Jesus and as it was in the earliest days of the life of the Church. In each of these cases, a new stage of history was opened up by God's call which in fact required that there were things to be left behind.

In the gospels, we find Jesus proclaiming the kingdom of God both in his words and in his actions. In his resurrection out of death, the kingdom of God comes about in him personally. And this resurrection is the promise of what God seeks do for all humankind.

The resurrection of Jesus was the climax of the presence and action of God in the history of Israel. It brought about the transition from the Old Testament to the New. It is the turning point into a new era of God's dealings with his people; in it the plan of God moved into a new key. One of the characteristics of this new time was the realisation that Christ's coming was not just for Israel but for all the peoples of the world. The group of Jesus' disciples – as we saw in the last chapter – had to leave behind their exclusive belonging to the Jewish people with the cherished customs and practices that were part of that and had to move on into the Gentile world which was not only strange to them but initially even repugnant as we can see in Peter's initial reaction to the thought of eating unclean foods in the house of Cornelius in Acts of the Apostles 10:1 to 11:18.

There were many elements of Judaism which those first Christians kept and which Christians still keep today. We continue to use the books of the Old Testament; we continue to pray the psalms which make up so much of the constant prayer of the Church. And we are still nourished by much of the spirituality, prayer and ideas which we have inherited from Judaism.

However, at the core of the Christian faith is the belief that Jesus was the promised Messiah and that he was not only for the Jewish people but for all humankind. This faith in Christ proved to be the decisive point of difference between Judaism and Christianity and from it so much else would gradually devolve. This difference and the transition it involved brought about the serious division in the very early Church itself which was discussed in the last chapter. The division centred on what was radically new in Christianity, what elements of Judaism were to be part of the continuing life of the Church and what elements were to be left behind. The evidence for this division is very evident in the Acts of the Apostles and the Letters of St Paul. It is also often in the background of passages of the gospels.

Leaving things behind

Leaving things behind is part of every human transition. It is true of the transition out of childhood into adolescence, and that from adolescence into adulthood, as it is true of moving into retirement. In leaving childhood, the child's relationship to their parents has to change as they move into adolescence and then into adulthood. The relationship to the parents is radical and constant but it has to undergo change if it is to continue to flourish. And that change has its challenges for both parents and children. If that change is rejected by either party, the relationship will be sorely damaged. If the child refuses to move on, they will remain something of a child and never take proper possession of his or herself. If parents refuse to accept the child's transition into adulthood, they risk either losing or infantilising their child.

These transitions in life are familiar to all human beings and illustrate a pattern of continuity in discontinuity which is integral to all significant human growth.

In the present time, the Church is immersed in a wide-ranging and radical transition which is affecting every dimension of its existence. The Second Vatican Council was the watershed in the Church's formal and decisive coming to grips with this transition. The transition was already taking place before that Council and it continues after it. Vatican II concluded in the mid-1960s but, in common with earlier Ecumenical Councils, the leaven which it kneaded into the batch of the whole Church is taking time to have its effects.

Vatican II's occurrence and documents are not the end of this process of transition but are its formal and ecclesially certified starting point. From them there has been and continues to be a domino effect. The opening up to contemporary society which characterised Vatican II is an ongoing process requiring constant discernment in prayer, study and pastoral experience. A process given renewed stimulus in the words and works of Pope Francis.

The acceptance of the basic thrusts of that Ecumenical Council is crucial for the health and wellbeing of the Church as it moves into the future. To refuse these basic thrusts is to move into a dead end.

There is a parallel between the refusal to accept the human transitions mentioned above and the refusal to accept the present transition in the life of the Church. Insecurity and fear are at work in both of these transitions. If the transition in the life of the Church is refused, its life will be distorted; it will become self-referential rather than open to the society to which it is sent by the gospel of Christ. Without this transition, the relationship between the Church and its members will also be distorted because the members of the Church are also members of the civil society to which they belong and so they tend to be influenced by the mentality of that society. If a due balance between Church and society is not kept, people's faith is in danger of being divorced from their lives; it will be like an addition to their concrete lives, rather than an integral part of it.

The refusal to enter into the present transition can also bring about a situation in which believers are faced with a choice between their faith and their contemporary mentality as members of the society with which they identify. In our congregations today, such a choice is already facing many people. This is especially true of many 'retired' members of the Church, for some of whom such a retirement is only undertaken with reluctance.

Clinging to the past out of insecurity or fear can reduce faith in God to a religious infantilism, which contradicts the call to conversion present throughout the gospels. That conversion is a call to go beyond ourselves. Clinging to the past out of a resistance to change for whatever reason risks turning the Church into an irrelevancy or a relic of the past.

In looking into the process involved in the Second Vatican Council, we can see that it was a process of coming to grips with new social and cultural situations within which the Church was living out its life and mission. Prophetically, the Council foresaw the need to take that new situation seriously and to enter into dialogue with it.

The break-through document of Vatican II on the Church in the Contemporary World (called *Gaudium et Spes*) was the document which specifically set out to reshape the Church's relationship to the societies and cultures of which it was part. In principle, it broke the Church out of the self-defensive attitudes which, at least since the French Revolution, tended to place the Church and society at odds with each other.[5]

---

[5] For a recent and thorough treatment of this situation, see John T. McCreevy, *Catholicism. A Global History from the French Revolution to Pope Francis*, NY/London: W.W. Norton and Company Inc., 2022.

The Council in all its documents, but most especially in the above mentioned document on the Church in the Contemporary World, set about creating different relationships with the much changed people and societies of contemporary times. That new relationship can be summed up in the word 'dialogue'. The proposal of dialogue as the way forward in the relationship of the Church and contemporary societies is also set forth by Pope Paul VI in his documents *Ecclesiam Suam* and *Evangelii Nuntiandi*[6] and is again brought into high focus and given new impetus in the major documents of Pope Francis.[7] Such a dialogue is not just a matter of strategy for the Church but an essential part of the Church's embodiment of the gospel in contemporary times. A parallel dialogue has taken place – even if only implicitly – in every age of the Church. In every age and in every place, the Church has lived in the larger context of the society to which it belonged.

And this dialogue has in every age had a formative influence on the understanding of the faith. It is not just a matter of external adaptation but of a renewed understanding and presentation of faith in Christ in the light of the new questions and issues raised by each age.

Faith is lived within time and circumstances

Change in our days is particularly challenging because of the shift out of formally religious societies into secular societies. For so many centuries, religion was part of people's natural social inheritance and it was lived as part of their social existence. There was little talk of evangelisation in such times because it was presumed that individuals would imbibe their religious tradition from their surroundings.

---

[6] Paul VI, *Ecclesiam Suam*, 6 August 1964; *Evangelii Nuntiandi*, 9 December 1975.
[7] Apostolic Exhortation *Evangelii Gaudium* (2013) nos. 238-258. (Henceforth referred to as Ev.G.)

Moving into the future does mean change, and it can be a difficult thing for people to do. To understand this difficulty more deeply, it is helpful to reflect on the concrete way in which most people have received and lived their faith over many centuries until recent decades.

Traditionally, the Catholic faith was lived concretely and practically as a dimension of the daily lives of believers. What it meant to people to be Catholic was embedded in their life experience which was the concrete, practical way in which they experienced their faith and their belonging to the Church. This was associated with and reinforced by experiences of liturgy, of various other religious practices, of family life, of belonging to a parish community, and, in most cases, of belonging to a particular nation or people which was Catholic. And that last element was particularly strong in forming Catholic identity as a dimension of one's social and cultural belonging to a particular people, which was the situation of most Catholics until the twentieth century.

Inherent in such concrete living and receiving of the faith is the natural tendency to identify one's particular experience of faith with the faith itself. Such a concrete and social reception and living of the faith is strongly embedded in particular times, places and circumstances.

Given people's living of their faith in concrete, particular circumstances, it is understandable that many would find it difficult to go along with changes to their way of believing. However, when those very same concrete circumstances of life are subject to substantial change, that change also affects people's adherence to their inherited faith. This was illustrated powerfully in the shift from the village way of life and its culture to an urban way of life and its accompanying culture which occurred in the movement of people out of their villages into cities in the course of the Industrial Revolution in the eighteenth and nineteenth centuries. Having left the village in which their practice of the faith was embedded, that practice changed significantly or disappeared altogether in their new social situation.

Today, there is a parallel to that change brought about during the Industrial Revolution. The faith of the recent past which was often embedded in strong ties between faith, culture and nationality is easily undermined when the transition occurs into a secularising society which no longer makes those links.

When such change is factually happening to us, a time of critical choice is opened up. Such change brings about a situation in which a choice needs to be made, a choice to move on into the new situation because the nature of the change is such that it is beyond the individual's control – and, for that matter, beyond the Church's control. It is simply happening. This is our situation today.

It was this social and cultural change that the bishops of the Second Vatican Council discerned; they became cognisant of the fact that they were dealing with an already changed social, cultural and political situation whose consequences were unfolding and would continue to unfold. The major changes introduced by that Council were a response to the changes already powerfully afoot and which were clearly going to shape the future.

It is a compliment to the faith of the greater part of the Catholic people that the changes following Vatican II come about with relative ease and acceptance.

It is also clear that the handing on of the faith in this new situation will not happen automatically as it did in the earlier situation. There needs to be an explicit entry of the gospel into people's lives if they are to become Christian.

Continuity in difference

An important element in the current transition is the awareness that in a Church which is universal, the experience of believers is different in the different cultures in which they live. The practical living out of the faith is different for Christians living in third world countries, as it is for those living in countries inimical to religion, as it is for people living in Islamic societies, as it for people living in completely Catholic countries such as Ireland or Poland or Malta once were. As it was different for Catholics who lived in a Catholic subculture as had been the case in England or Australia. And for Catholics in the West today, it will be different as they live within secularising cultures.

However, once people come into contact with others who have lived their faith in a different place and time, and within a different culture, they can begin to see that the way they have lived their faith is not the only way to do so and that their own way of doing so has been shaped by the culture and circumstances in which that way has been embedded.

As said above, in a completely Catholic or Christian situation, the fact that almost everyone has the same faith tends to give that faith the status of being a fact of life. That faith becomes part of the common sense of such a society; it shapes the way that society sees the world. Whereas in a situation in which faith and culture do not easily coalesce, such faith is no longer part of the accepted common sense of the society. Believers are thrown back upon themselves and their explicitly believing communities for support.

It is also clear that new questions about their faith arise within believers themselves by the very fact that they live in a non-believing society and are part of families all of whose members are no longer believers.

Differences over time

The same recognition of a diversity in the ways of believing and practising the Christian faith comes about when we compare our present time to past times. The particular way in which contemporary believers live out and practise their faith is not just a copy of what believers have done in every age of the Church's life. There are differences in mentality, practices and theology in different ages of the church. Present believers would not necessarily find it easy to fit into the ways of Catholic communities as they were in earlier periods of history.

This discovery of such continuity in difference represents one of the great thrusts of the Second Vatican Council. This discovery was based on a great deal of historical work preceding the Council, which involved a re-discovery and a new appreciation of the history of the Catholic Tradition. This studying of history discovered that there have been a variety of rites, practices, devotions and theological approaches to the Christian Mystery throughout the long history of the Christian Tradition.

There have also been rituals and devotions and theological approaches which have arisen at particular times and places and have then faded and disappeared. There have also been approaches to the Christian faith which have distorted the understanding and practice of Christianity and these have been formally set aside.

The studies of the history of the Scriptures and the Tradition have also laid bare a continuity rooted in the person of Christ which links all the different periods together.

Thus it is that the two major thrusts of Vatican II join forces – the recovery of an understanding of our past in its continuity and differences, which in turn enables us to clear the ground of unnecessary ideas and practices and so establish a dialogue with the changed societies of present times, which is the other central thrust of the Council, which John XXIII called 'aggiornamento' – a word meaning 'bringing things up to the day'.

The past and the future

The realisation that the history of the Christian tradition is based on a continuity of faith in different contexts, cultures and circumstances means that everything that was part of our past does not need to be carried forward into the future. The discernment of what we carry forward and what belongs specifically to an earlier stage of the Church's life – and so needs to be left behind – requires careful discernment both pastorally and theologically. It takes time and growing insight and the emergence of a consensus within the Church for this to come about. This consensus is promoted by significant moments in Christian history such as Ecumenical Councils. In the current transition in the life of the Church, there have already been changes which involved leaving things behind which were part and parcel of a previous stage of the Church's history and which even seemed to be part of Catholic Identity.

I would like to give some examples of such changes: specifically, the use of the Latin language in the liturgy, the particular shape of the Church in the period following the Council of Trent (1545-1563) and the inherited parish structure which is undergoing change in many parts of the Catholic world today.

The Latin language

An obvious example of something which in principle has been left behind in recent decades is the use of the Latin language in the liturgy. The use of Latin had been determined by many historical circumstances. For instance, the fact that for many centuries Latin was the only commonly written language in Western Europe and was the *lingua franca* of those who were literate. Other languages were gradually emerging in Europe but they were, for the most part, at an unwritten stage of development and were, by and large, dialects tied to particular localities in the various countries we now call Europe. Latin was the language of the clergy and at that time the liturgy was considered to be their business.[8]

In addition to the above, following the Reformation, the use of Latin became one of the signs of being Catholic over against being Protestant. As a result, the use of Latin was cobbled to the idea of the universality of the Catholic Church, that is it was seen as a sign of the unity and universality of the Catholic Church over against the many forms of Protestantism.

---

[8] For a fuller treatment of this, see Frank O'Loughlin, *Gathering the People of God*. Bayswater: Coventry Press, 2020, 39-47.

In our time, new circumstances have arisen which have undermined all of the reasons for the use of a Latin liturgy. A new level of education has arisen among the people of the Church. There was and is a growing movement towards seeing the liturgy as a matter for the whole People of God rather than just a matter for the clergy, a movement canonised by Vatican II and its subsequent documents. And, of course, there are now the many languages of the people in which the liturgy can find fine expression.

The use of Latin in the liturgy also fell into line with the inward looking attitude of the Church which followed the French revolution and its conflicts.[9] The use of the languages of the people for the liturgy is an element in the opening out of the Church to the contemporary world.

Also the ecumenical movement looked more closely at those things which Catholics and other Christian Traditions had in common rather than those that separated them. Thus the Latin liturgy was no longer seen as a sign of Catholic identity and in fact came to be seen as a burden to the ongoing life and flourishing of the Church.

We still have those who grasp on to the use of Latin as a means of holding on to the past and delaying or avoiding change.

The form of Catholicism after the Council of Trent

Another important element to be reckoned with in looking at our present transition and the movement forward of the Tradition is the particular historical shaping that was given to the Church over the last four and a half centuries by implementation of the decrees of the Council of Trent (1545-1563). These decrees were a boon for the Church at that time. That Council introduced an era of reform and renewal in the history of the Church which set the Church on a new path by comparison to the preceding centuries.

---

[9] See McCreevy as above.

The Council of Trent was concerned both with the reform of the Catholic Church in those matters which were failures and abuses in the later Middle Ages and also with the defence of Catholic doctrine and practice against the doctrines and practices set in place by the various Protestant Churches. This issued in an era in which Catholics and Protestants were very often defining themselves by their opposition to each other. This opposition formed the religious mentality of the era: Catholics wanted to distinguish themselves from what Protestants did or thought and Protestants wanted to distinguish themselves from what Catholics did or thought. This mentality had a strong influence on the theology and practice of both protagonists.

In the course of the re-discovery of the Scriptures and the Tradition during the nineteenth and twentieth centuries, it was shown that the above Post-Reformation doctrines and practices had a shape and a rootedness in their own particular time, culture and circumstances which were not present in either the Scriptures or the earlier phases of the Tradition. These studies provided the opportunity for all Christian denominations to begin to look at what went before them and to compare their own approaches to those present in the other stages of the Christian Tradition. This was an invitation to all Christian traditions to go beyond their own way of seeing things and to begin to find common ground between them and to look for common pathways ahead.

Restructuring of parishes

Since the Council of Trent, the parish has been the basic local structure of the Church. There were, of course, parishes before that Council but following Trent, it was seen as the basic structuring of the Church and became one of the main focuses of the reform of the Church and of its activity and mission.

However, in many places today, this basic structure is having to undergo restructuring because of basic practical changes in the

Church's ongoing life. In the first place, the scarcity of priests means that many parishes which once had their own priest pastor and enjoyed their due autonomy as individual parishes can no longer do so. This has brought about the situation in which several parishes may be joined together to form one parish or a cluster of parishes is formed with one priest serving them all. This shift has not proved to be an easy one. Long-standing parishes tend to have their own ethos and their own particular sense of identity and often do not find it easy to integrate with other parishes.

The initial presenting issue behind this need for restructuring is the scarcity of priests but the more telling issue is the scarcity of people in parish congregations. There are clearly fewer people coming together to celebrate Mass on Sundays. There are several reasons for this but I would suggest that the major reason is something frequently spoken about in this book and that is the fact that the Church is now part of a secularising society which is having its strong influence on the membership of the Church.

For particular local churches to be viable, there needs to be a sufficient quorum of members for the Church to be able to be the Church in all its dimensions and to be able to respond to Christ's call and fulfil its mission.

The hard work of combining communities requires a sense of conversion everyone's part – a willingness to go beyond our inherited situation. It requires the leaving of comfort zones and a readiness to move into a future which may be found uncomfortable - at least for a while. This is a very practical issue and also an unnerving issue of the contemporary moment in the life of the Church.

This issue constantly arouses calls for married men to be ordained priests and for the ordination of women to the priesthood. This constant call which comes so frequently from the People of God needs to be listened to.

***

The point of the above examples is that the practice and understanding of the Faith is influenced by the circumstances within which it is lived out. When those circumstances change, the influence which they had is no longer relevant to the living of the Faith in the new situation. And so a new form of the same Faith comes about, and elements which belong to that earlier form of the Faith are no longer important or even relevant and so need to be left behind.

Past and future today

In the life of the Church today, the issue of what is to be carried forward and what left behind is both important and troublesome. In the wake of Vatican II, there are those who want to cling to the past or even return to the past as they imagine it to have been.

Some such people refuse to accept the Second Vatican Council and the renewal set in train by it; others probably just want to cling to the old ways without necessarily taking an explicit stand against the Council.

However, the attitudes underlying these stances manifest an understanding of the Church at odds with that proposed in the documents of Vatican II and, for that matter, at odds with the centuries-long stretch of the Catholic Tradition. This is no small matter. Ecumenical Councils have a particular way of seeking a consensus and therefore have always been understood as a means by which the Holy Spirit influences and guides the Church.

To reject the Council is to put oneself in the same position as those who have rejected such Councils in the past. It is to put one's own particular understanding of the Church and the Christian Mystery before that which has been discerned in the process of a solemn gathering of the Church in Council.

There may be all sorts of psychological, sociological and political issues involved in the choice to ignore or oppose such a Council. However, the call to conversion and movement into the future which is part of the long biblical tradition can never be excluded from what it means to be a Catholic Christian. The call of conversion which is the call to go beyond ourselves and our way of thinking and living is always present for the Christian believer of whatever shade of opinion. Vatican II made such a call to the whole Church and most responded to it to the best of their ability despite the difficulties that some may have felt.

With regard to those who simply cling to what they have known, this attitude raises questions about what faith really means. Christian faith cannot simply be a salve to human insecurities and fears; that is to say it cannot be just a form of 'opium of the people' as Karl Marx would have had us believe; nor can the Christian faith be simply a matter of 'Here I stand' in parallel to Martin Luther's taking up his religious position. The call to conversion – to go beyond ourselves – is an unavoidable element of the Christian faith.

Christian faith has to have that characteristic which we saw in the life of Abraham, in the Exodus from Egypt, in the Exile of Israel from their land, and supremely in the life, death and resurrection of Jesus, and then following on from him, in the experience of the first Christians. That characteristic involves a movement into the future, buoyed up by faith in the God who opens a way ahead for his people, however threatening their surrounding difficulties may seem to be.

Today's exodus

Living in the Church today, we can see various positions being put forward regarding the shape of the Church's future.

We can see those who, both in practice and in understanding, are moving into the future as a new era in the life of the Church. They see themselves as a responsive to and a specifically Christian part of the society to which they belong. This arises out of the conviction that Christ must be proclaimed in the new societal context of today. They do so in the belief that in the process they themselves will discover new depths to the gospel[10] and that such contemporary dialogue can open doors to the gospel in contemporary cultures. Pope Francis is a firm example of such a stance.

We can also see that there are those who do not want to move into a new future at all but who are determined to keep everything as it has been. This is often based on a reading of history which sees only an unchanging continuity and does not take into account the diversity which has actually been part of that continuity. In the holding of such a position, neither culture nor context is taken into account. Culture or context is seen simply as something external to the living of the faith, which is seen to exist at a level of its own, untouched by the history and the culture in which it exits.

Then there are some who find that they are unable to find their way ahead and who therefore find themselves paralysed in their position. This can be particularly problematic when it concerns those in leadership positions in the Church.

The central thrust of the life of the Church requires a fundamental attitude of moving ahead into the future into which we are being called. Change is demanding; it tests the depth of faith. Change can make people question their beliefs and their identity as Catholics or Christians; it can also lead to the maturing of faith. The historian John O'Malley speaks of the importance of change with regard to identity in this way: "Change engenders identity, but it is also a condition for maintaining it by acting as a remedy for ossification and irrelevance".[11] Note that O'Malley is suggesting that change actually *engenders* identity, that is that it ultimately brings about a renewed and deeper sense of our identity as Christian believers.

---

[10] Ev.G. 11.
[11] John W O'Malley, 'Reform in the life of the Church', in Antonio Spadaro and Carlos Maria Galli (eds) *For a Missionary Reform of the Church*. The Civillta Cattolica Seminar, NY/Mahwah, NJ: Paulist Press, 2017, p. 77.

The Christian faith and the Christian Church are part of human history and include everything which is part of being human. Human history moves on and is subject to constant changes both small and great. We cannot stall history at a stage that suits us and treat that stage of history as the way things ought to be. We can all be subject to the temptation to live in the past, but it is perilous to allow that temptation to prevail or be institutionalised. It would indeed lead to what O'Malley describes as "ossification and irrelevance".

It was such an orientation to the past that Pope John XXIII – historian that he was – and the Fathers of the Second Vatican Council saw happening in the Church of their time. They saw it as not connecting sufficiently to contemporary people and their living issues. The Council's perception is well expressed in John XXIII's word "aggiornamento".

One of the most significant discoveries of the theology of the nineteenth and twentieth centuries was that we have to be aware of the influence of history if we wish to have an adequate understanding of anything human, including the Church and its theology and practice.

In his apostolic letter *Evangelii Gaudium* (The Joy of the Gospel), Pope Francis states that it is not good enough to say, 'We have always done it this way'.[12] Our past ways are embedded in past times and those times have indeed passed. They will not and cannot return! History cannot go backwards.

---

[12] Ev.G. 33.

Chapter Four
WHAT IS TO BE LEFT BEHIND?

There is a useful image in nature for the transition which the Christian faith is passing through at the present time: snakes shed their skin, but the same snake lives on in a new skin, which was already being formed under the old skin. The new skin is formed out of the snake's very substance; it is part of its nature to produce such new skin. The skin is not just a clothing; it is part of the snake's interaction with its environment and the climate of the various seasons of the year. So it is with the Christian Tradition. It is the faith of a believing People who live in different times and have different cultures and the same continuing faith in Christ becomes incarnate in those times and cultures.

The new 'skin' of the Church in our time has been in formation under the old 'skin' for quite a long time. The new one belongs to the Church quite as much as did the old. Neither 'skin' is external to the Church but has been formed as part of its existence and presence in the world of its time and culture. Just as the new skin of the snake came about by means of the workings of the internal biological dynamics of the snake, so significant changes in the Church come about by the internal spiritual workings of a living faith in the People of God in each time and culture. The Holy Spirit constantly inhabits, enlivens and energises the People of God.

The Church moves on in history and keeps rediscovering itself as that history moves on. That rediscovery enables it to leave behind what is no longer relevant to its continuing presence and mission. It is leaving behind what would in fact be a hindrance to its presence and mission in a new time and context precisely because such things were formed in dialogue with a past time and context.

Such change is not just a matter of finding new means of communication for the same message but of entering into a dialogue with contemporary human beings and their society. In the course of which dialogue that contemporary situation can become fertile ground for the gospel. Such dialogues can unearth new aspects of the gospel which will manifest its constant capacity for newness and relevance.[13] The specific elements of Christianity that earlier dialogues with other cultures had evoked become part of the accumulated treasury of the Catholic Tradition but are not a suitable means of embodying the gospel in a new cultural situation. This dialogue goes on not only between believers and other members of society but also within and between contemporary believers themselves.

A significant historical example of such a cultural dialogue was the transition from a theology attuned to the Jewish background of the Scriptures to a theology more attuned to the world of the Graeco-Roman Empire in the third, fourth and fifth centuries of the Christian era.

In the New Testament, we see Christ being proclaimed with reference to the texts of the Old Testament and Jewish tradition. Christ was presented as the Messiah who was expected by Israel, who had been foretold by Moses, the prophets and in the psalms. What happened to him and in him was "according to the Scriptures".

Once the Church moved into the Graeco-Roman Empire, it was engaged in a dialogue with different peoples and cultures who knew nothing of the Old Testament. So we find in that new situation that the revelation of God in Christ was being presented in terms which arose in the dialogue with the world of Greece and Rome. This dialogue was not only happening between the

---

[13] A point made strongly by Pope Francis in Ev.G. 11.

Christian thinkers and others in that society but within those Christians themselves since they were believers in Christ who shared the culture of their time.

It is out of this dialogue that we became used to such terms as nature, substance and person to explain Christ and the Trinity. This is the terminology that is to be found in the Nicene Creed used at Mass. This creed arises out of the proceedings of the first four Ecumenical Councils: those of Nicaea (325), Constantinople I (381), Ephesus (431) and Chalcedon (451). These Councils remain a point of reference for all the mainline Christian Churches.

In the New Testament situation and in the era of the early Councils, it was the same Mystery of Christ that was being presented in two different Christian dialogues, in two different contexts, in two different 'languages'. And the new context of the Graeco-Roman world drew out aspects of the Christian faith which were inherent in the earlier phase of tradition.

Prayerful and careful discernment was required in each of the above dialogues so that the Mystery of Christ could be genuinely proclaimed. There could not be a Christian 'takeover' of the culture of the time or a cultural 'takeover' of the Mystery of Christ. In each of the above dialogues, that with the Old Testament and that with the Graeco-Roman culture, there were misinterpretations of the Mystery of Christ which had to be avoided.

As time went on and Christianity became more widely accepted, the preaching of the gospel in that new context of the Roman Empire was also related to the preceding religious culture of the peoples of the far flung Roman Empire. Christ was presented as revealing the true and different God over against the gods of the past. There is a beginning of this in Paul's speech to the Athenians on the Areopagus in chapter 15 of the Acts of the Apostles. Paul speaks to the Athenians not in terms of the Old Testament – as he did when speaking to Jewish people – but in terms of revealing the unknown God. He did this on the basis of his discovery of an altar to the unknown god as he walked around Athens, thus linking what he had to say into their background and culture.

And in our own times?

Coming to our own times, what do we need to carry forward? What do we need to go beyond? And so, what do we need to leave behind? I don't think that we can yet answer those questions comprehensively; we have to let the process of transition keep moving on and discern attentively the signs of our times in the light of the life of Jesus Christ and of the good news he proclaimed. It is already clear that there are things that we cannot but leave behind. Some suggestions follow.

The presumption of faith

We can no longer *presume* that people generally believe in Christ or in God; this is true even of those who have been brought up in the Christian faith. Many people do believe but in secular societies we cannot work on that as a presumption. Even for those who are believers, there is a need to speak to the unbeliever in the believer because believers themselves belong to and are influenced by the secularising cultures in which they live.

    The gospel needs to be proclaimed anew. The effective handing on of the gospel involves paying attention to people's capacity to receive the gospel which is being handed on to them. It requires that we present the gospel in terms that are in tune with people's embedded understanding of human life and of the world in which they live. This underlies today's frequent talk of evangelisation which is a prominent topic pastorally, theologically and in the formal documents of the Church. Entering into this new era of the Church's life requires an understanding that the handing on and receiving of the gospel is to be at the forefront of *all* that we do. Consequently, people's personal and cultural situation has to be taken into account if they are to be able to receive and respond to the gospel personally and with conviction.

    As background to this new situation, I would like to recall what was said earlier in this book about the long term historical situation in which Western cultures moved from being formally and legally Christian to their being secular and pluralist. In that earlier situation everyone within the society was considered Christian, and if they were not, it was thought that they should be. This grew out of the conviction that the gospel had already been handed on and embedded in those societies and so there was really no need to keep up an initial proclaiming of the gospel but rather to attend to its explanation and expansion. Those who did not accept the gospel were treated with suspicion if not worse. That situation falls back on the fact that Christianity and society were tightly woven into each other.

Obviously, such an arrangement between religion and society is no longer the case in the secularising and pluralist societies in which so many Churches exist today. Rather, the gospel has to be handed on anew.

There are initiatives of renewal being promoted today which do not take this changed situation sufficiently into account but rather seek to arouse a dormant or implicit faith that they believe is present within people. Such initiatives can have some immediate results in people still influenced by the earlier situation of religion and society but I do not think that they can have long-term effects in those brought up within a secularising society.

On the other hand, it is certainly possible to call upon the deep desires of the human heart and invite people into the discovery of the God who made human beings in his own image and seeks to bring them to himself. But we can no longer work on a presumption of a widespread explicit or latent belief in God in the people of secular societies.

A liturgical presumption

Emphasis on evangelisation is most important when it comes to liturgy, and especially when it comes to the Sunday Eucharist which is the nerve centre of liturgy and for that matter of the life of the Church itself.

When those who gather for Mass belong to a secularising and pluralist society and are therefore influenced by it, the celebration of the liturgy itself needs to address that situation and be imbued with an evangelising attitude. It needs to be weaving together the lives and culture of the people gathered and the gospel of Jesus Christ.

In the past, the prayer, the symbolic forms and the understanding of the liturgy worked on the presumption that the liturgy was being celebrated with people who were in principle already evangelised or who had an established Christian belief. That is a presumption that can no longer be relied on.

Of course, the liturgy is always the celebration of the death and resurrection of Jesus Christ and all evangelisation moves towards that Mystery. And it is the liturgy's task to open up a space of dynamic tension between the gathered people and the Mystery of Christ into which they are being continually evangelised. It is in this space that the evangelising role of the liturgy fits. There is, therefore, a dialogical dimension to the liturgy not just in the interplay between the people and the priest and other ministers but, in its very nature, the liturgy is an interplay between those gathered and the mystery into which they are being drawn. It seeks to reshape human existence in terms of the words, actions, and death and resurrection of Jesus Christ.

The liturgy, like Christianity itself, is essentially incomplete; it involves an ongoing, life-shaping process. On the one hand, of its very nature, it celebrates the coming of Christ while looking towards the completion of that coming in the future. In the Eucharist, we celebrate Christ's death until he comes (1 Corinthians 11:23-27).

On the other hand, the gathered community is gradually taking to itself the Mystery it is celebrating, a process that will only be completed when Christ's coming is complete. The gathered community is in the process of becoming Christian, a process that is, in principle, incomplete.

Incompleteness is an essential aspect of the liturgy. This point is made by the liturgy itself and it does so with special poignancy in the celebration of the Easter Vigil. The Easter Vigil is not the celebration of the completion of God's plan in the resurrection of Jesus. It is notable that the very first note in the Roman Missal speaking of the Easter Vigil, says: "By the most ancient tradition, this is the night of keeping vigil for the Lord (Exodus 12:42), in which, following the Gospel admonition (Luke 12:35-37), the faithful, carrying lighted lamps in their hands, should be like those looking for the Lord when he returns, so that at his coming he may find them awake and have them sit at his table".[14] Even on that most holy of all nights, the Church is aware that what it celebrates is incomplete. The whole People of God lives in the tension between what has already come about in Christ and its promised fulfilment, yet to come.

Likewise, the whole season of Advent is filled with the call to Christ to come again because the Kingdom of God which came about in his resurrection has so obviously not yet come about in the Church let alone in the rest of humanity. Advent is the season of calling on the Lord to keep coming and complete what he has begun.

The celebration of the liturgy cannot be a closed, complete and unchanging circuit as if it has already come to a completed state. This is so because of the very nature of Christianity as incomplete. As such, it also has to be open to the real situation of the people celebrating it and the circumstances of their lives. Its celebration needs to be a handing on of the good news of Jesus Christ, which can only happen in an exchange with those celebrating it. The texts and symbolic forms of the liturgy need to be open to the understanding and participation of those who are gathered for its celebration. This implies an openness to the culture and mentality of those celebrating the liturgy in order that they may be taken up into the Mystery they are celebrating.[15]

---

[14] *The Roman Missal*, The Easter Vigil in the Holy Night, no 1.
[15] See Pope Francis, Apostolic Letter, *Desiderio desideravi*, 2022. London: Catholic Truth Society, 2022. (Henceforth referred to as D.d.)

Participation

In contrast with the practice of many centuries past, communicability is now seen as a matter of great weight in the celebration of the liturgy. What mattered in the period prior to Vatican II was that the liturgy was celebrated correctly in accord with the rubrics and there was little concern for the participation of the people. The liturgy was seen to have its effects irrespective of the direct involvement of the people present at the celebration. It was the priest who celebrated the liturgy; the people attended the liturgy which it was the priest's role to celebrate. As a result of this approach, the proclamation of the word was seen as unimportant and the involvement of the people in the actual celebration of the liturgy fell by the wayside; even receiving communion was seen as, at best, a rare event for the people. The priest fulfilled his liturgical role and in parallel to the priest the people who were present prayed in whatever way they choose. In principle, the roles of priest and people did not intersect.

A Church centred on itself

The recent abuse crisis has had terrible consequences for the victims of the abuse and for their families and supporters; it has also had grave consequences for the Church in terms of its reputation, and of the disillusion which has led many people to dissociate themselves from it. It was not just the abuse itself that caused this turmoil but, even more so, its cover up by Church authorities. It was the cover up which proved the more disillusioning for people both inside and outside the Church.

That cover-up was most often motivated by the desire to protect the Church and its reputation. This featured so strongly in the mentality of the time that it blocked out the capacity to see the evil that was being done to innocent children and fragile adults. It was a mentality that clouded an authentic sense of right and wrong.

This attempt to cover up instances of abuse brought into the light an attitude that pervaded much of the life of the Church and can continue to do so. It brings out into the light an attitude that considered the good reputation of the Church as the most important value to be served. And, at a deeper level, it gave expression to a view of the Church as centred upon itself, a Church turned in on itself.

Such self-centeredness, such a self-referential attitude, is a malaise in the life of the Church. It is a contradiction to Christ's call to his disciples to go beyond themselves which is the very meaning of the word conversion.

There is some history to be taken into account in this concentration of the Church upon itself. The European Enlightenment of the 18th century and the Church's overall reaction to it began to create a new era which was re-enforced by what occurred in the French Revolution and its imitation in other countries. A certain disdain for Christianity arose and this disdain at times turned into violence against those who were part of the Church. By and large, there came to be a great deal of antipathy between those who followed the Enlightenment and those who were part of the Church. Both the Enlightenment and the playing out of the French Revolution made clear the Church's loss of power in the age that was coming into being in comparison to the age that was ending.

The above movements brought about a reaction of self-defensiveness in the Church, both among the people of the Church and among its leaders. It was expressed in many of the papal documents of the 19th century under Pope Gregory XVI and Pope Pius IX. With regard to the Church and the general society of the time, it was as if there were two worlds living beside each other in unease and often in conflict.

Over against this situation of the 19th and early 20th centuries, the Second Vatican Council and the popes in its wake called for a Church going out of itself, a church concerned with what is beyond itself.[16] The Council, and echoing it, the recent popes are calling

---

[16] Ev.G. 19-33.

for a Church which does not remain within its own boundaries in a need to find security but which moves out of its comfort zone and its defensiveness into a more open future. The call is for a Church which, like Abraham our father in faith and Israel in its Exodus out of Egypt, and the Church of the New Testament, sets out on a new path which is not secure and safe but which has to be undertaken step-by-step and in trusting faith. It is a new path which can be disturbing and frightening but on which the Church needs to move ahead. The whole People of God is being called to follow its Master, Jesus Christ, into a journey into a future which is not clearly known but which it enters upon by entrusting itself into God's hands.

There are two aspects to this exit or exodus out of the Church's inherited situation. There is the movement out of the self-protective attitude into an openness to the society in which the Church is called to exist. And then there is a movement out of a past – seen as more secure – into a future which may be glimpsed but is not definite or assured.

Along with this new openness, the recognition of the Church's very real humanity and capacity for sinfulness is necessary for the very credibility of the Church. Transparency and authenticity have a power to inspire human beings in all walks of life and become even more impressive over against the instances where such is lacking. For the Church whose whole raison d'être is based in Jesus Christ and his gospel, it is even more important. Transparency is necessary if the Church is to be seen as being authentic.

The present transition in the life of the Church cannot be "kept in order" or tidied up. Even though we are in a process which involves continuity-in-difference with the rest of the tradition, it takes time for that continuity to emerge and for the differences to be discerned. We are in a situation in which we are feeling our way ahead step by step, and it is crucial that we are open to the new possibilities which the entry into this new stage of our history offers. The process cannot be short-circuited.

Clericalism

In his words and actions, Pope Francis names clericalism as a malaise in the life of the Church. He sees it as an obstacle to the Church's future flourishing.

What is meant by clericalism? Clericalism is a particular manifestation of the Church's centeredness upon itself. As the word implies, it is first and foremost about attitudes among the clergy but such attitudes can be part of an overall attitude within the whole Church.

As an attitude among the clergy, it is about seeing the Church as embodied in the clergy, that is seeing the clergy as "the real Church" and the people as, in principle, dependent on and secondary to the clergy. It tends to reduce the Church to the ordained ministers. At its worst, it gives the clergy an undue sense of their own importance and treats the ordained ministries not as ministries of service but as sources of honour and power.

This clericalism is manifested in the liturgy as one would expect. The liturgy was regarded in the past – and is still regarded by many – as the affair of the clergy in which the people join at a subsidiary level.

Over against that attitude, the description of the Mass given in the Introduction to the present Roman Missal is significant. Whereas the pre-Vatican II liturgy described the whole Mass in terms of the priest' words and actions; the present liturgy sees the Mass as the action of the whole people of God. The description of the Mass in the present Missal reads as follows: "At Mass or the Lord's Supper, the People of God is called together, with a priest presiding and acting in the person of Christ, to celebrate the memorial of the Lord or the Eucharistic Sacrifice".[17]

This description of the Mass presents the whole People of God gathered together as its celebrating subject. The priest's role

---

[17] *The General Instruction of the Roman Missal*. Strathfield, NSW: St Pauls Publications, no. 27.

is named and circumscribed; it is to preside over the gathered assembly, and to do so as one significant sign among others of Christ's presence and action. The priest has a particular and essential role within that gathering of the Church but the primary subject of the celebration is the whole community of faith.[18] This changes the focus of the celebration of the Eucharist quite radically by comparison to the description of and presumptions behind the pre-Vatican II Missal. It is hard to avoid the conclusion that that earlier understanding of the Mass and the role of the priest in it lies behind much of the present opposition to the liturgy reformed by Vatican II.

A highly significant manifestation of clericalism in the liturgy is the practice of the people receiving the Eucharist by means of hosts taken from the tabernacle, rather than hosts consecrated at the Mass which the community is celebrating, whose high point is the reception of communion. By contrast, if a priest were to receive communion from the tabernacle at Mass, he would be seen as not having celebrated Mass at all! In traditional terminology, he would not have participated in the sacrifice of the Mass because he did not receive communion from hosts involved in the action of that Mass.

Surely that same principle applies to the people who gather, with a priest presiding "to celebrate the memorial of the Lord or the Eucharistic sacrifice". Have they participated properly in the action of the Mass if they have received communion from the tabernacle? This practice betrays the fact that the people are not seen as celebrating "the memorial of the Lord or the Eucharistic Sacrifice". It is the most significant and disturbing manifestation of clericalism because, by and large, it is taken for granted and hardly noticed. And it has such a long history in the practice of the Church! It embodies the notion that it is the priest who really celebrates the Mass, rather than the whole People of God, who are the Church!

---

[18] Yves Congar, 'The Ecclesia or Christian Community as a whole celebrates the Liturgy' in (ed.) P. Philibert, *At the Heart of Christian Worship. Liturgical Essays of Yves Congar*. Collegeville, Md.: Liturgical Press, 2010, 15-68.

The priest is not the Church. The whole gathered community including the priest is the Church.

The issue of clericalism has consequences for the question of vocations to ordained ministry. Much of the promotion of vocations invites people to be part of the Church as it once was. It tends to ignore the reality of a Church in its contemporary and quite radical transition. And this transitional state will continue to be the case into the foreseeable future. The present forms of the promotion of vocations often tend to elicit a response from those who are looking backwards and who are seeking a restoration of the past. They appeal to a certain type of mindset and psychology which is of very questionable value for the Church's future.[19]

In being realistic about the present situation of the Church, does not the call for vocations to ordained ministry and religious life need to be cast in terms of building the Church of the future? A Church capable of dialogue with the concrete society in which it lives, which is the context in which members of the Church live their lives? Would not such an approach strike a chord with a wider variety of possible responders?

Preoccupation with numbers

One of the concerns of most contemporary Churches in Western societies is falling attendance numbers. Falling numbers is not just a matter of having fewer clergy and religious but, even more significantly, of there being fewer people gathering together for the celebration of the liturgy. The community of the Church is

---

[19] In regard to vocations, the following telling comment was made by the French theologian, Joseph Moingt: "Our society has ceased to be religious, it no longer needs religion as it tries to identify itself or to function or to project itself into the future. This is the deeper cause for the decline in clerical vocations: our society no longer produces priests because it no longer wishes to reproduce itself according to the religious model in which they were symbolic actors." (Actualité des ministres, *Recherches de Sciences Religieuses* 90 (2002) 224.

decreasing numerically. This is not happening universally but it is happening very noticeably in those countries which were once formally Christian but now have a secularising and pluralistic culture.

Even though this cannot but be noticed and it does have quite serious consequences, reactions to it are often fraught with unhelpful anxiety. We cannot let such anxiety dominate our way into the future.

There is a variety of reasons why people no longer participate regularly in the life of the Church. There are people who are aggrieved or disillusioned but there are also large numbers who do not see the point of being part of the Church, who simply do not see how faith or belonging to the Church fits into their lives. And then for some, the basic question is whether believing in God makes sense at all. Yet others retreat into a faith which is purely individual with little or no connection to any form of faith which is communal.

This leads us to two crucial points both of which have been already mentioned several times in this book. First, there is the need to recognise that contemporary people are *in the first instance members of* a secularising society which is, to some extent at least, shaping their mindset; and secondly, that faith has to be presented in a way that finds leverage within their view of life. This requires an account of 'the hope that is within us' as the First Letter of St Peter puts it (3:15-16), or as the Letter to the Colossians puts it when advising people on their approach to those who do not believe: "Your speech should always be gracious, flavoured with wit, to know how you should give an answer to each individual' (4:4-6).

The faith as it was presented to people two generations ago will not have the impact on people today which it had at that time.

Faith, science and fundamentalism

One of the issues which is a hindrance to people's coming to faith today is the commonly held opinion that there is a significant conflict between faith in God and a scientific worldview. In principle, there ought to be no conflict but there is in the minds of many people.

The mentality of many contemporary people is very strongly influenced by the considerable achievements of the both the natural and the human sciences. There are contemporary thinkers and scientists – but by no means all – who hold religion in disdain and even seek to promote its demise. Contemporary Church documents insist that there ought to be no conflict between religion and science, so long as neither exceeds the horizon of their specific fields. Neither religion nor science should intrude on what is the proper field of endeavour for the other.

For believers, there ought to be no separation between the realm of the sciences and the realm of religious faith; although there needs to be a clear distinction between the two so as to give to each its proper autonomy. As Christians, we believe that our universe and the human minds seeking to understand that universe are gifts that come from the One who is the fountain of all life in its wonderful variety, creativity and capacity to evolve.

A significant problem giving rise to unnecessary conflict between faith in God and science and contemporary thought in general is a persistent fundamentalism in the interpretation of the Scriptures. Fundamentalism ignores the fact that the Scriptures are always the word of God in the words of human beings[20] and treats the Scriptures as if they had come straight from the mouth of God without any mediation.

To understand the Scriptures, one must also take into account the human beings who wrote them. They were human beings who lived in their own culture and times. The biblical authors are the people who mediate the word of God to us, doing so from within their own context and culture.

---

[20] Vatican II, *Constitution on Divine Revelation, Dei Verbum*, nos.11-13 (Henceforth referred to as D.V); Benedict XVI, Apostolic Exhortation *Verbum Domini*, Strathfield, NSW: St Pauls Publications, 2011, no. 29.

An adequate interpretation of the Scriptures has to take into account the original context in which each part of the Scriptures was written and the human authorship involved. It also needs to take into account the considerable diversity that is present within the Scriptures themselves. The scriptural texts which we have were written over a long stretch of time and in quite diverse circumstances. There is a process of development and refinement in the understanding of God and the things of God embedded in the Scriptures themselves.

A significant example – relevant to our present discussion – are the stories of the creation of the world which in the past have been a source of conflict between science, historical studies and religion. For a start, there are two stories of creation which were written at different times and by different authors and which tell differing stories.

In reading the first creation story (Genesis 1:1 to 2:4), the author describes the creation of the world in terms of what the human eye can see which was the basic means by which people of that time understood the universe around them. They described God's creation of the world in terms of the world as they saw it.

In the second creation story (Genesis 2:5 to 3:24), we have a story centred on the situation of human beings as created by God and yet as separated from God. This story uses the symbolic resources available to the author to speak of the human situation and its present relationship with God. It speaks of human beings as earthenware creatures who yet bear the breath of God within them. It is a highly symbolic narrative whose meaning cannot be discerned without understanding such symbols: a garden, a tree of life, a snake capable of speech, God walking in a garden, nakedness, man and woman scapegoating each other.

Our context today is very different to that behind the first creation narrative. We now have the means to discover dimensions of the world of which the people of that time could not even have dreamed. What the creation story is expressing is that the living God is the one who gives the world its being. In parallel, we believe that the world as we know it today is the world to which God is constantly giving life. It is the same faith in the creating and life-giving God being expressed in two different human contexts, in two different mentalities.

Our context today is different to that of the second creation narrative as well. To a great extent – because of the scientific mentality of our times – we have lost the capacity to live with the symbolic dimension of life which is so prominent in that second narrative. In recent times, there has been an unfortunate tendency to interpret it literally. We are only gradually rediscovering the capacity to live with and understand symbols which are so much a part of so many other cultures.[21]

What is true of the creation narratives which I have here used as an example is true of all of the Scriptures: they are written by people inspired by God but that inspiration occurs within their particular time and culture.

Working together

Different perspectives on the world produce different approaches to the complex reality of our world. Each perspective has something to bring to the overall understanding of the world we live in. One perspective cannot take over the role of all the others; each has to have respect for what other approaches bring to light. Religion cannot take over from science or history nor can science or history take over from religion. Each has to be given its proper space and recognition; none of them has the right to be totalitarian. As will be explained further on in this book, the theologian Yves Congar speaks of 'cognitive minorities' in our societies.[22] That is, there are groups of people within our societies which have a particular insight into reality or have a body of knowledge which they have for the

---

[21] See Pope Francis, D.d. 41-45.
[22] Y. Congar, *The Word and the Spirit*. London: Geoffrey Chapman, San Francisco: Harper and Row Publishers, 1986, p. 127 (Congar takes this concept from sociology).

good of all. This is a useful idea in understanding the Church's role in contemporary society.

The Church is one such cognitive minority. The body of scientists is another such cognitive minority. Each cognitive minority has its own specific contribution to make to the whole and should not intrude on the role of other such groups, much less exclude them from consideration. Scientists, philosophers, historians, artists, believers all fit into this category of cognitive minorities, and each has its contribution to make to the overall understanding of our world, and the functioning of our societies.

A false start: Christianity reduced to morality[23]

In any time of transition, there can be false starts – that is ways of trying to move ahead which end up fruitless or lead into dead ends.

One such false start is the common understanding of Christianity today as merely a form of morality. Christianity does indeed have an essential moral dimension involving the following of Jesus Christ, but it cannot be reduced to that moral dimension. This moralising tendency has been present from the eighteenth century on and was given considerable credence under the influence of the philosopher Emmanuel Kant. Kant actually saw this reduction of religion to morality as a way of giving meaning to religion. In the course of the intervening time, that way of thinking has become commonplace.

This reduction of Christianity comes down to seeing 'being a Christian' as the same as 'being a good person'. Christians are indeed called to be good but that does not describe their specific identity. It reduces Christianity to its moral dimension. Such a reduction omits the core reality of Christianity which is the discovery of God in the life, death and resurrection of Jesus Christ.

Every religion, worldview or ethical system sets a particular path to what it sees as goodness, it encourages a way of life which is in

---

[23] Ev.G. 34.

accord with its particular view of life and what it sees as the good. Such views of goodness are not just a matter of personal, subjective intentions and activity but are a matter of established values and attitudes which the particular tradition seeks to knead into the workings of the society to which it belongs and into the lives of the individuals who are part of it. To take a simplistic example, we can see in capitalism and in communism two different systems with very different sets of values and attitudes which they seek to establish and promote in the societies in which they are influential. Each sees some things as good and some things as evil. There are very practical consequences of all such determinations of what is good and what is ill.

Each culture and tradition has its own set of values and attitudes which it seeks to inculcate. Christianity has its own particular set of values and attitudes and its own particular view of goodness and evil which grounded in the life of Jesus Christ. From his life and death there arise particular paths towards goodness as there are recognised evils to be avoided.

To claim that being good is the equivalent of being Christian is to ignore the goodness that has its own particular shapes in other religious and ethical views of the world. Goodness is not only to be found in Christianity. And goodness found in other traditions has to be recognised as belonging specifically to those traditions. From a specifically Christian point of view, the silent work of the Holy Spirit can be seen at work in all manifestations of the good, wherever they appear; but they are not the same in each tradition.

Christianity has its meaning and purpose in its relationship to Jesus Christ which also determines the particular shape of Christian morality. Later in this book, we will be looking in detail at the specific shape of Christianity and its claim to uniqueness.

This reduction to morality can also be an aspect of attempts to reduce the many traditions of humanity to a common denominator. Such attempts would lose the richness and variety of the vast diversity of human beings and their traditions. The choice of such a common denominator is usually in accord with the mindset of those proposing it and often without regard for the views of those inhabiting other traditions.

What actually occurs in formal, inter-religious dialogues is a deepening appreciation of and respect for each partner's religious tradition and a deeper grasp of and commitment to one's own tradition. The differences between traditions are real and are a matter of strong convictions; they are not to be glossed over but appreciated and pondered more deeply.

Another false start: return to the past

As we saw earlier on, there are those who, faced with the current transition in society and in the Church, see the solution as going back to the way things were. Restorations of the past are simply impossible. The past has indeed passed and the course of history shows that it is impossible to restore it. In fact, any attempt at restoration of the past is strongly concentrated on a negative dialogue with the present precisely because it is trying to escape it. This is so because the very act of the attempt at restoration arises out of encountering and wishing to bypass a new and different situation; the attempt at restoration is being shaped and determined by the current changing situation which those promoting the restoration fear.

Chapter Five

WHAT WILL THE FUTURE HOLD?

The question posed in the title of this chapter is – in a true sense –unanswerable. But we have learned from history that in every age new attitudes and movements have arisen which become part of the woof and weave of new and differing times which eventually came to be.

Above, we have looked at the nature of transitions and have seen that in their course there are things which need to be left behind. We have applied this insight to the present transition through which Church is moving.

We now need to take into account some of the specific issues being presented to the Church in this new epoch. We need to look at some of the particular characteristics of this time, characteristics that Church as a whole needs to take into account. What are those things which constitute the specific challenges of this new epoch?

Signs of the times

Such questions as those above bring up the issue of the 'signs of the times'. The reading of the signs of the times is a thread which the Second Vatican Council and subsequent popes have woven into the life of the Church.[24] The signs of the times are those attitudes and movements characteristic of a particular time or culture to which the Church needs to pay attention and to do so in the light shed on them by the gospel of Jesus Christ in order to find in them an echo of that same gospel. So we seek to let the life, acts and words of Christ shine on these attitudes and movements in order to discern in them indications of the workings of God in our present world.

Reading the signs of the times in the light of the gospel is an aspect of the pastoral conversion to which Pope Francis is calling the whole Church and especially theologians.[25] The culture and historical situation of human beings at any time in history is the theatre of the Church's presence and responsibility; it is the arena in which the Church is called to make the gospel present, that is to let the light of Christ shine in it.[26] Taking the signs of the times seriously is never just a matter of ascertaining that they are matters of concern in a society but of looking at them in the light shed by Christ and the tradition stemming from him in order to discern the presence and stimulus of the Holy Spirit who is always at work in this world that carries the imprint of the creating hand of God. That imprint remains, even when it is distorted by human insufficiencies and sinfulness.

Reading the signs of the times is not just something recent in the life of the Church. We can see its equivalent in the New Testament. Many of the passages in the gospels and other parts of the New Testament have to be interpreted in terms of the issues and situations of the time of Jesus and the New Testament writers. Those writings came about within the context and conditions of their times. Matthew, Mark, Luke, John and Paul were each writing

---

[24] Vatican's Document on the Church in the Contemporary World 4. (Henceforth this document will be referred to as G & S); Ev. G 51,108.
[25] See Apostolic Letter of Pope Francis *Ad theologiam promovendam* (New Statues for the Pontifical Academy of Theology). Issued on 1 November 2023.
[26] L.G. 1; G & S, 1; Ev.G. 52, 108.

with an eye on specific situations of the people for whom they were writing, the world in which they were living.

We can see some specific instances of this. When the expectation that Christ would return very soon after his death failed to be the case, those first Christians had to learn to read their time differently, to see the life of the Church differently. That delay was a 'sign' of a new and different time within the life of the Church itself.

Then again, when non-Jews began to respond to the gospel of Christ, they read in that the sign of a new epoch in the life of the Church, an epoch in which it would be explicitly directed to all the nations of the earth. And they came to that decision in the light of texts of the Old Testament which spoke of the gentiles coming to God. That is, they read this as a sign in the light of the Scriptures.

The above two 'signs' concern the life of the Church in its relationship to the world in which it was existing. Our reading of the signs of our times is parallel to their reading of the signs of their times. Each of them is tied into the relationship of the Church to the times in which it was being called to live and to proclaim Christ.

★★★

Besides naming the signs of the times, it is necessary to understand how the Church is called to be present in the world. This can be summed up in an image that Pope Francis frequently uses for the Church: the image of a field hospital which he presents in contrast to the image of a court house. The Church is called to be in the midst of all the ups and downs of human life and struggle as a place of consolation and healing, rather than as a place of judgment.

The engagement with the changing world of our time is a process; it cannot simply be done and put behind us. It is not simply a matter of making a decision or writing a document; nor can the time span needed for the process be determined beforehand. It is an ongoing process in which both the members of the Church and its institutions continue to engage. It is itself part of the ongoing process of epochal change; it is a process afoot in the emerging world of which the Church is an integral part. The Church and Christians generally have a particular and irreplaceable contribution to make to this emerging world: Jesus Christ and his gospel.

Emerging signs of a new time

As we have already seen, one of the keys to evangelisation is dialogue – a dialogue in which each partner to the dialogue is accorded respect and an attentive hearing. This can be difficult when there is an already conflicted situation in which those in the discussion have become hardened in their views and their opposition to each other. Many such discussions need a fresh start.

The issues named below are some of the characteristics of the times into which the Church is entering; they are issues with which the Church needs to engage to be true to itself. It will not be sufficient to approach these issues with ready-made answers which come from outside of the ongoing engagement with them. Simply, pre-packaged responses have little capacity to be convincing. Respectful dialogue is required and can prove productive.

This implies not only that the issues arising be taken seriously but that the Church's tradition be taken seriously. To take the Church's tradition seriously means that the various historical contexts and the formulations of the gospel appropriate to those contexts need to be thoroughly studied and their significance in the contemporary situation discerned. As Pope Francis says, the gospel cannot simply be transmitted in already determined formulae.[27] The same gospel of Jesus Christ finds diverse expressions and formulations as it is embedded in different cultures and contexts.

---

[27] Ev.G. 129.

The major sign of our times

There are issues unique to our times – not just passing issues but issues that quite clearly will stretch into the future and be constitutive of that future.

The most significant of these issues is the very nature of contemporary Western societies as secularising and pluralist. We have already discussed this several times in the course of this book. This is a major thread of the change of epochs in the course of which we are living our lives. As the shift from the biblical world to the Graeco-Roman world brought about a different presentation of the Mystery of Christ, so today, Christian engagement with the secular and pluralist world will bring about another presentation of the same Mystery.

Given some of the thinking and attitudes of secular and pluralist societies, their approach to some issues will be something with which Christians will not be able to agree. This will bring about discussions which will need to be conducted in mutual understanding if not always in agreement. Dialogues which produce acrimony come to a dead end rather than producing understanding and respect. It is only understanding that can lead to some possibility of movement ahead on disputed issues.

Particular signs of our times

There are particular issues which are signs of our times that need to be taken up in the onward movement of the Church into the new epoch. Some of these issues are mentioned below, but as time moves on, we need to be alert to other issues that may emerge.

In this book, there will be no attempt to deal with these issues in detail. For anyone wishing to follow up on these issues, there is an abundant and accessible literature available on each of them.

The place of women

Even before the question of women in ordained ministry is considered, there is a critical need for serious engagement with women and particularly with the women of the Church. Their contribution to the life of the Church is immeasurable and their critique of the ways of the Church is often sharp and needs a serious response. Such a new relationship between women and the Church cannot be mere tokenism – as is sometimes the case. In fact, such tokenism betrays an underlying misogyny and/or a failure to grasp the importance of the issue. Without sincere engagement with women, the Church is, as it were, trying to walk on one leg. Today, the inclusion of women in the workings of any organisation is increasingly a question of that organisation's credibility. And so it is for the Church.

The Synod on Synodality in Rome has already moved ahead with the inclusion of women, in that women for the first time in the Church's history are voting members of the synodal process.

Gender and sexuality

The issues surrounding sexuality and gender pose huge and soul-searching questions for the Church. They are issues which involve the Church's credibility in the eyes of contemporary women and men, including believing women and men. Many members of the Church have ceased listening to the Church on issues of sexuality and marriage because the Church's words too often do not engage with their real questions and, at times, seem to have the ring of unreality about them.

In the background to all issues of sexuality and gender, there is required a solid reconsideration of the Catholic tradition and the contexts in which much of that tradition has been formulated. Already there has been solid and positive work done on these issues both theologically and pastorally.[28] Here again, simply pre-determined responses to questions of sexuality and marriage do not have weight in the contemporary situation. Without genuine listening and self-searching responses, the Church will not be heard or even listened to. This does not mean that our tradition has nothing to say on these matters but it does mean that that tradition has to be re-examined and discerned in the light of genuine and sincere contemporary questioning.

Ecology and climate change

Whether people agree with it or not, it is impossible today to be ignorant of the question of climate change and its effects on the stability of the planet. It is a vital question concerning the future of the whole human family. It is a question that has been addressed by recent popes and has been raised insistently by Pope Francis in his letter *Laudato Si'* and his consequent document *Laudate Dominum*[29] This is an issue which goes way beyond the scope of this book, save to state the reality and seriousness of it, and also to acknowledge the capacity of the human mind and human creativity to deal with such considerable issues once they are taken seriously.

The Church as Catholic

We live in a global world and this requires that the catholicity of the Catholic Church be real. As has often been said, it can no

---

[28] We can see some indication of this work in the following authors: John Mahoney, *The Making of Moral Theology*. Oxford: Clarendon Press, 1987; James F Keenan, *A History of Catholic Theological Ethics*, NY/Mahwah NJ: Paulist Press, 2022; Charles E Curran & Lisa A Fullam (eds), *The Sensus Fidelium and Moral Theology*, NY/Mahwah NJ: Paulist Press, 2017. And for those who read Italian, Andrea Grillo, *Cattolicesimo e (omo)sessualita*, Brescia: Schole (Morcelliana),202. Note especially Pope Francis' document *Amoris Laetitia*.

[29] Pope Francis, Encyclical Letter *Laudato Si'*, 2015. Strathfield, NSW: St Pauls Publications, 2015.

longer be a 'Roman-centred' or 'European-centred' catholicity but needs truly to reflect the Church as a worldwide communion. This immediately raises the vital issue of the inculturation of the faith in the many cultures in which it exists. It involves what can be called trans-culturation. This word makes the point that there has never been a stage when the gospel was outside of a culture; it has always – from its earliest Jewish times – been imbued by a culture. Moving into a new culture means that it has to move from one cultural context in which it has already taken form into another cultural context in which it is taking form. In this book, we have already discussed such a transition in the movement of the Church out of the biblical and Jewish world into that of the Graeco-Roman Empire.

Such a change is already underway in the Church as we see in the current emphasis on the relationship between the centre of the Church and its peripheries, with a new insistence on the real participation of those on the periphery. It has also taken very concrete form in the makeup of the College of Cardinals whose members now reflect the presence of the Church in almost every part of the world.

Authority and status

Another sign of the present times is that authority and status can no longer be simply taken for granted or seen as unquestionable and definitive. There is a keen desire for authenticity and for transparency in all areas of life and this is especially so with regard to the exercise of authority; when these qualities are missing, scepticism and cynicism predominate among people. Thus forms of authority need to be backed up by a moral authority both in institutions themselves and in the persons having authority within those institutions. Statements intended to carry authority need to be accompanied by the clear presentation of the reasons behind whatever decision is put forward.

This can be a significant problem in the Church if those in positions of authority – at whatever level – cling to their position without being open to opinions expressed in the wider Church and/or in the society to which the members of the Church belong.

Andrea Grillo, a prominent Italian theologian, takes up the thoughts of the renowned Canadian Catholic thinker, Charles Taylor, and speaks about a shift in our times from a society of honour to a society of dignity. In the society of honour, there is an inbuilt inequality in terms of degrees of honour attributed to people who have status in the society without regard for their personal qualities. Such people of honour were kings, the aristocracy, the bishops, and also priests. Such societies were tightly hierarchical. In the society of dignity – in principle at least – the dignity attributed to each person creates a basic equality of all and looks for a personal responsibility in all.[30] This has considerable repercussions for the use of authority in our present culture and in the Church.

Spirituality

Earlier in the book, there was mentioned the fascinating fact that in societies which are as secular and secularising as most of those in the Western world today, there is a rise in the search for spirituality among many people. This is a sign of the times which is of great significance for the Church. We cannot ignore the persistent recurrence of the deep desire in human beings for the spiritual and for what gives meaning to human life. A greater opening up of the treasures of the Church's spiritual traditions would seem an obvious means of developing the spiritual urges in human beings and of opening them up to God. There will be more on spirituality in a later chapter of this book.

---

[30] Andrea Grillo, *Cattolicesimo e (omo) sessualita*. 139. For the work of Charles Taylor see: *The Malaise of Modernity*, Toronto: Anansi Press, 1991 and *The Ethics of Authenticity*, Cambridge, MA./London, England: Harvard University Press, 2018.

The human and technology

The dignity and sanctity of human persons is a fundamental principle of the Christian faith and so issues concerning the human person will always be crucial in Christian public engagement. Along with this, there is now much discussion about the capacities of artificial intelligence and the prospect of the artificial replacement of multiple organs of the body. The question arises: what exactly makes the human to be human. To speak adequately on this issue is way beyond the scope of this book but it is today a live issue and requires appropriate theological and pastoral attention.[31]

'Technological' is one of the words used to describe our age and it reflects the developments in technology which could not even have been imagined just a decade or so ago. This technology has its great advantages as well as creating problems, but is a significant aspect of the world into which we are moving and it cannot be overlooked if the Church is to be present and relevant in the contemporary world.

***

The above signs of the times raise a selection of issues of which the Church needs to be aware as we enter a new epoch of human history. They are issues which are already being raised within the Church and which call on the Church for a response. Such a response needs to be grounded in the gospel of Jesus Christ, and this requires serious reflection and discussion. We are at the beginning of this process.

---

[31] See Lieven Breve, Yves De Messenger and Ellen Van Stichel (eds), *Questioning the Human. Toward a Theological Anthropology for the Twenty-First Century*. NY: Fordham University Press, 2014.

Part 2
What do we take with us into the future?

INTRODUCTION

The Christian faith – as its name suggests – is centred on Jesus Christ. Relationship to him is what makes people, places and institutions Christian. This relationship can take many forms and it comes about and develops in different people and situations in different ways but the focus of anyone or anything Christian needs to be on Jesus Christ.

In times of cultural and religious transition like our own, the clarity of this focus becomes even more important. When people have questions about what it means to be Christian, or cannot see the point of being Christian, the presentation of the Christian/Catholic faith needs to be more precisely focused on the centre from which all its other aspects flow; it needs to be strikingly clear that Jesus Christ is the heart which pumps life into every dimension of being Christian. In times of deep change, we need to go to the source from which Christianity springs.

In this time when the whole Church is being called upon to renew itself, we need to sharpen and deepen the focus on Christ. Only in this way can we gain a true sense of our own authentic identity. Pope Francis expressed such a focusing in an interview recorded in *L'Osservatore Romano* in 2014. His words were: "For me, the greatest revolution is to go to the roots, to recognise them and see what those roots have to say today".[32] Focusing on Jesus Christ is to go to the roots of the Christian faith. In his document written as the Church was entering the third millennium, John Paul

---

[32] *L'Osservatore Romano*, 20 June 2014, p. 6.

II states the same principle in saying that we must start again from Christ.³³

Along the same line of thought and taking it further, we find Pope Francis writing in *Evangelii Gaudium*: "Whenever we make the effort to return to the source and to recover the original freshness of the Gospel, new avenues arise, new paths of creativity open up, with different forms of expression, more eloquent signs and words with new meaning for today's world. Every form of authentic evangelisation is always 'new'" (no. 11).

Going to the core

A passage in the Acts of the Apostles provides us with a way to name those things that we need to carry forward into the new age into which we are being called. Referring to the first Christians, we read: "These remained faithful to the teaching of the apostles, to fellowship, to the breaking of the bread and to the prayers" (Acts 2:42).

These four things to which those first Christians were called to be faithful are the same things to which Christians today are being called to be faithful. For us, these four things are to be found in the New Testament (the teaching of the apostles), the community of the faithful – the Church (the fellowship), the Eucharist (the breaking of the bread) and in prayer (the prayers).

In these four things, we can identify the life supports which we need to carry with us on our journey into the future. They keep us in touch with the Christ who is at the heart of our faith. In the course of the long history of the Christian faith, these things have had to be clarified and expanded because new situations have arisen or because of misrepresentations of Christianity, but they do offer us a useful way of getting to those core things which Christ and his

---

[33] John Paul II, *Novo Millennio Ineunte*, 2001. Strathfield, NSW: St Pauls Publications, 2001, 29.

first disciples have left us and to which we are always being called to be faithful.

These four things do not exhaust the full expanse of the Christian faith but they do give us the means of access to its core: Jesus Christ himself. From these four things, there are derived further essential aspects of the Christian faith. Then there are other aspects of the faith, which may be beliefs, practices or attitudes, which do not have the same centrality or importance in the Christian faith. There is a hierarchy among the many dimensions and doctrines of the Christian faith.[34]

---

[34] See Vatican II, Document on Ecumenism, *Unitatis Redintegratio*, no.11; Ev.G. 36.

Chapter Six

FAITHFUL TO THE TEACHING OF THE APOSTLES

In hearing the phrase which is the title of this chapter, our minds probably tend to go immediately to the books of the New Testament and to the gospels in particular. This is as it should be. However, the New Testament needs the Old Testament because it testifies to the tradition within which the New Testament came to birth and the New Testament in its turn brings the Old Testament to completion in Jesus the Messiah.

We have become increasingly aware that the Christian tradition was in existence before the New Testament was written down. As the document on Divine Revelation of Vatican II states, the apostles handed on "by the spoken word of their preaching, by the example they gave, by the institutions they established, what they themselves had received – whether from the lips of Christ, from his way of life and his works or whether they had learned it at the prompting of the Holy Spirit".[35]

This living tradition was gradually consigned to writing. It found expression in the letters of the apostles, in the four gospels and in the other writings of the New Testament. This concrete written form was crucial to preserve the authenticity of the tradition beyond the time of the original witnesses and to act as a means of authenticating what belonged to the tradition and what did not.

---

[35] D.V. 7.

In the New Testament writings, the words of Christ and those of his first witnesses echo down to us in this twenty-first century.

Christ and the New Testament

Each of the gospels is written backwards! That is, they were written because of and in the light of Jesus' resurrection out of death. This discovery of Christ alive after his death was the spark that lit the fire of Christianity. Under the influence of the Holy Spirit, the first Christians could see that there were tentacles reaching out from the Old Testament towards Jesus Christ and his death and resurrection.[36] This was the reason for the statement that what had happened to Jesus was "in accordance with the Scriptures".[37]

Again, if we look at the preaching of Peter after Pentecost in the Acts of the Apostles, what he is proclaiming is the resurrection of Jesus. And likewise in the letters of St Paul, nothing makes any sense without faith in the extraordinary discovery of Jesus alive after his death. "If Christ is not risen, our faith is in vain." (1 Corinthians 15:16) In Paul's inimitable way, that phrase says it all.

In death is life

The resurrection is not a resuscitation. It is not about returning to human life as we now know it. It is about life beyond life as we now know it.

The death and resurrection of Jesus is often called the Paschal Mystery. This phrase falls back upon Old Testament imagery. The word 'Paschal' comes from the Hebrew word for Passover and

---

[36] In the light of Jesus' death and resurrection, such texts as the following are seen as pointing to Jesus' death and resurrection: Psalms 15, 30, 90, 109, 117; Isaiah 42:1-9; 49:1-6; 50:4-11; 52:13 to 53:12.

[37] See Luke 24:25-27, 32, 44; 1 Corinthians 15:3-9. Note that this phrase also appears in the Nicene Creed used at Mass.

originally refers to Israel's being led from slavery to freedom in the Exodus out of Egypt, which – at the time of Jesus and still now – is celebrated at the Jewish feast of Passover.

This image of the Passover is applied to the death and resurrection of Jesus. It is used as an image to enable us to see into the meaning of that death and resurrection. It enables us to see that Jesus' death and resurrection is a passing over, a transition, from life as we know it now through death into the fullness of life with God. It is about a Passover into life beyond anything we can now imagine. It is being born anew. It is a new act of God opening a way before his people and indeed before all humankind.

A good image for this Passover – of this new entry into life – is to take up and develop the New Testament image of new birth. If we think of birth from what we might call the baby's point of view, then we could say that, if a baby could think, its birth would seem to it to be its death. It would think that it was coming to the end of the only life it has ever known – life in the womb.

But as we know, the baby is not coming to the end of its life but to the beginning of a life more wonderful than it could possibly have imagined from the womb – life as we know it in all the wonder of the world in which we live. Such is the new birth brought about by the passover of Jesus through death into life. This image is a light which enables us to catch an echo of the future that is promised to us in the death and resurrection of Jesus.

Just as the New Testament is written in the light of the resurrection, so the Christian life is lived in the light of the resurrection; it is a call to live as if there is no death.

Bearing the marks of his death

The risen Lord appears to his disciples bearing the marks of his death (John 20:19-29). He has not simply skipped over death; he has suffered death and has come to life in that death. Because of this, death is no longer the ultimate enemy of human beings, but has become the way into life. A power stronger than death has entered into the world in the person of Jesus Christ.

That is, in his relationship to the Father who is the source of all life, Jesus brings that new life from God into the human world. That life is such that death is swallowed up by it. The in-flow of life into our world from the very source of life is such that death cannot resist it.

The death of Jesus is of crucial importance. As a human being, he died as all human beings must die. But, as we saw earlier, his death was brought about by political, religious and popular forces which were powerful in his time. Such forces were not just powerful in his time, but are powerful in every time and continue to bring about suffering and death in every time and place. His death came about by the same combination of forces which had brought about people's death before him and have continued to bring about death among human beings right down to our own days. He encountered the death-dealing powers which are at work among human beings.

What killed Jesus Christ? Who killed Jesus Christ? There was a co-ordination of forces which brought him to his death. Pontius Pilate had his crucial part in his death – despite any protestation of innocence by the washing of his hands; the religious leaders had their part in his death, the mob had their part, his own disciples and especially Judas Iscariot had their part. The general expectation in Israel of what the Messiah ought to be like blinded people to the true Messiah when he came. The human desire to want what we want and be blinded by that desire had its part. Jesus asked them to go beyond the way they thought and what they desired and they could not do it.

All these people involved in the death of Jesus are simply instances of attitudes and actions which are constantly at work among human beings and continue to bring death and diminishment upon other human beings. How many other instances are there of Pilate's ambition? Of leaders wanting to be rid of someone who undermined their political arrangements? Of crowds taking on murderous attitudes? Of human blindness which refuses to open its eyes?

The death and resurrection of Jesus is about every human life and every human situation. It is about releasing human beings from the forces of evil which are at work in our history and lives. It is about the setting free of human beings from the ultimate influence of evil and from death as the end of life. It is about taking the life-ending power of killing out of the hands of those who kill!

Jesus' resurrection is God's taking Jesus' side in the conflicts between him and those seeking his death. This is not just about an ancient Roman Governor and first-century Jewish leaders and one particular mob but about everyone who holds power over others and about those powerful urges and forces which are within human beings and which can be aroused to great evil.

In the opposition to and the consequent discarding of Jesus Christ, we see an epitome of human sinfulness at work; we see the distance and separation of human beings from God which is a dimension of the human condition.[38]

In the strangest of ways...

But this victory of God over evil and death happens in the strangest of ways. The entry of God into the world in the person and life of Jesus works in its own God-like way. There is no violence, no clear vanquishing of evil, no obvious victory over evil and death. The 'baddies' do not get their proper desserts. God does not show them who is boss! We are dealing with the Holy One who will not resort to human violence to achieve his purpose – despite the cost! This is the God who will not add to the human violence which is so evident in our world.

---

[38] Human sinfulness is a reality of our human condition which needs to be better understood in the presentation of the Christian faith. See my earlier book *Does Sin Matter?* (Bayswater, Victoria: Coventry Press, 2022), for anyone who wishes to follow up on the understanding of sinfulness.

This is the God whom the New Testament names Love (1 John 4:7-10). This is the One whose ways are as high above ours as the heavens are above the earth. This is the One who makes his sun to shine on the just and the unjust and his rain to fall on the good and the bad (Matthew 5:43-48). There is no revenge in God, no capacity to hate, no desire to put human beings in their place! This is the One before whom so much of human reckoning is at a loss! This is the One who in Jesus Christ, shows us that he would rather be violated than be violent!

Christ the image of the unseen God

In Christ, St Paul tells us, we have the perfect image of the God we cannot see (Colossians 1:15). What is more, it is in Christ crucified and risen that we have the perfect image of the God who cannot be seen with human eyes and whose ways are beyond the workings of the human mind.

All the religions of the ancient world, with which the first Christians were surrounded, had images of their gods in the statues that filled their temples and their street shrines. Israel was forbidden to have such images because the only image God had given of himself were human beings made in his image and likeness.

In Christ, that image has become the perfect image of the living God. It is in the life, words, actions, death and resurrection of Jesus that we can find an echo of God showing us Godself. This image is, of course, a refracted image of God because in Jesus Christ God is immersed in our humanity. We cannot know God as he is in himself but only in his refracted reflection in Christ who is God-in-flesh, God-with-us, God embedded in our humanity.

The image of God we have in Jesus Christ is that of a human being who has been rejected, has suffered, has died on a cross and is risen out of that death. This is not the sort of image of the gods that human beings have had through all the ages of human religiousness. No human being dared to think that God would be as Jesus Christ reveals God to us. This is the God of total self-giving. This is imaging a God who gives himself to the point of death: his body given for us, his blood shed for us!

As we saw in the first part of this book, God keeps opening a way before his people and, in Jesus Christ, he has opened a way through death and death-dealing for his people and for all human beings.

Misleading images of God

The question of the image of God is a crucial matter for our times. There is a plethora of images of God in people's minds and in our culture, our literature and our art. So many of these images have been inherited from the past, without great attention being paid to their quality. Sometimes talk about God – both from believers and nonbelievers – can sound more like philosophy or ancient paganism than Christianity.

The word 'God' is in itself imageless and so is prone to picking up whatever feelings or attitudes or ideas about the divine that are implicitly present in people's minds or in the milieu around them. This matter of the common images of God that are lodged in people's minds is highly significant in seeking to present faith in Christ in our days. The undermining effect of misleading images of God is a major concern in making Christ's gospel known.

There is – as said earlier – a process of refinement at work throughout the Scriptures as they move towards the coming of Christ. And a similar process of refinement needs to be at work in the minds of those who have accepted the gospel and in those to whom the gospel is presented. Throughout the history of the Christian faith, there has been a constant need and effort to refine human thinking about God by reference to Christ and the gospels which bring his life, his words and deeds down to all the generations of the People of God.

The earlier section of this chapter on Christ as the perfect image of the unseen God is our constant point of reference for this purification and refinement of our understanding of God.

The world is already God's

The coming of Christ into our world needs to be placed in the wider context of God's presence among all human beings and in all of the universe. The very existence of our world is given to it by God who is the fountain of the life which is in all that lives and of the existence of all that is. He is, we may say, both father and mother of all that is. Christianity does not arise outside of our world but profoundly within it; it is the revelation of what lies at the source of our world and at its heart.

To go further into this relationship, I would like to begin with a consideration of the opening verses of the New Testament Letter to the Hebrews. These verses read: "In many ways and by many means in the past, God spoke to our ancestors through the prophets, but in these last days he has spoken to us in his Son, whom he appointed heir of all things and through whom he made the ages. He is the reflection of God's glory and the imprint of God's own being, sustaining all things by his powerful word" (Hebrews 1:1-3).

In these verses, the author is concerned with the relationship between God's word spoken throughout the Old Testament and his word embodied and spoken in Christ. The author of the Letter relates the two while making clear the pre-eminence of the word of God spoken and embodied in Jesus Christ.

In our situation today, there is a parallel to the situation described in the Letter to the Hebrews. We can relate the many ways in which God has made himself known to human beings throughout their history and the full revelation of Godself in the person of Jesus. We believe that God has been mysteriously at work "in many ways and by many means" among all human beings and in all religious traditions, while holding unreservedly that in Christ we have the ultimate revelation of God.

God's mysterious workings have not just been present in the past but are at work now, giving life and seeking to draw all human beings to God.

Believing in Jesus Christ involves the acceptance of God's presence and activity among all human beings but sees in Jesus an unprecedented and ultimate coming of God in a human being, and among human beings. Believing in Jesus Christ accepts the presence of God wherever it may be found and acknowledges that his followers can learn from those who have discovered God differently.

God's coming in Jesus Christ has the utter concreteness of God becoming a human being. This involves a presence of God among human beings which is unique to the Christian faith. No other religious tradition has this belief. It is this faith in Christ which gives Christianity is uniqueness and creates a different view of humanity and the world which is specifically Christian. The Christian claim is that this presence of God in Christ reveals at the deepest and most intimate level the God who gives life to all things. In Christ, God gives witness to himself in human flesh and in him, God is revealed as self-giving love.

The gift of faith

As we have seen, the real starting point of each of the gospels and the motivation behind their being written is the death and resurrection of Jesus. In his resurrection out of death, in his life beyond death, the Kingdom of God which he proclaimed during his life came about. The resurrection is not just an event in Jesus' life but is his life crystallised and brought to completion.

Faith in the resurrection brought the initial followers of Jesus – and those who have come after them – to believe that in him, God has come among human beings personally. And that in Jesus Christ we see God made visible. Visible not as God is in Godself but in the contours and reality of a human life and within the historical and cultural limits that are essential to that being human. In him, as St John's gospel proclaims, God in his Word has become human.

In this concrete man Jesus of Nazareth, Christians believe that God can be found. Ultimately, this faith comes about not as the result of a logical process or by human initiative but by means of an inner movement of God's Spirit. Peter's confession of faith is a model of this coming to faith (e.g. Matthew 16:13-18). Peter's faith came about not because 'flesh and blood' had revealed it to him but from the Father in heaven. It is because of this internal movement of God's Spirit that those first believers and contemporary believers proclaim Jesus Christ as Lord and source of life.

The core and the whole

Speaking of the death and resurrection of Jesus as the core of the Christian faith uses a telling image: core. In fruits, it is the core of the fruit with its seeds that gives the fruit its capacity to propagate, its creativity, its capacity to continue. So it is with Jesus' death and resurrection. It is the creative core of the Christian faith.

This faith in Christ has found expression in a series of truths, the most central of which are expressed in the Apostles' Creed and the Nicene Creed which are used in the liturgy. These creeds are not exhaustive of all the aspects of the Christian faith, but they crystallise that faith's basic understanding of God.

It is in these creeds – and particularly in the Nicene Creed and the Ecumenical Councils that gave rise to it – that the nature of God as the one God in the three persons of Father, Son and Holy Spirit finds expression as central to and characteristic of the Christian faith. This essential aspect of the faith arises from the presence of Jesus Christ as a human being in whom God personally reveals himself. Faith in the Trinity arises straight out of faith in Jesus Christ.

There are priorities among the various truths which express the overall Christian faith. And the proper understanding of these priorities is crucial to the credibility of the overall reality of Christianity.[39] All the various aspects of the Christian faith derive from Christ's person, words, death and resurrection. This is true both of those aspects which are of primary importance and those which are less so.

As an example, the Sunday celebration of the Mass is central to Catholic Christianity in particular and the reason for its centrality is Jesus' resurrection. The Mass is, above all else, the celebration of Christ's Passover through death into life. Sunday became the specifically Christian religious day over against the Jewish Sabbath because it was on that day, the first day of the week, that Jesus was discovered alive after his death. Likewise, the resurrection is the reason why the greatest feast of the Christian year is the Easter Triduum which celebrates his death and resurrection over the three days of Holy Thursday, Good Friday and the Easter Vigil of Holy Saturday and Easter Sunday.

Given the nature of contemporary secularising societies, the Christian faith will make sense by presenting what gives that faith its true identity and significance and what it means for being human. It is only by bringing to the fore what actually makes Christianity Christian that it can be understood and appreciated.

So there is no point in talking about the Mass – important as it is – unless it is understood in the light of faith in Jesus Christ and his death and resurrection.

It is the same for an understanding and acceptance of the Church. It has to be clearly related to Jesus Christ to find its meaning and purpose. It cannot justify its existence apart from him.

The same is true of veneration of Mary, the mother of Jesus. Appreciation of her role in the Christian faith can only come about once the person of Jesus himself is appreciated. The long tradition

---

[39] In more theological terms, this is referred to as 'The Hierarchy of Truths', as was mentioned earlier.

constantly presents her as the mother of Jesus and anything else said about her falls back upon her unique relationship with her son.

The same is true of Christian morality. It is always by reference to Christ that attitudes and values can be called Christian.

Passing on the teaching of the Apostles

There are already developments discernible in the handing on of faith in Christ within the writings of the New Testament. We have already spoken about the historical shift out of the original Jewish context of Christianity into the pagan world of Greece and Rome.

Looking into the gospels, we can see that each of the gospel writers proclaims their gospel with a particular group of people in mind. As the *Catechism of the Catholic Church* puts it: "The sacred authors, in writing the four gospels, selected certain of the many elements that had been handed on, either orally or already in written form; others they synthesised or explained with an eye to the situation of the churches, while sustaining the form of preaching, but always in such a fashion that they have told us the honest truth about Jesus".[40]

So Matthew's gospel is clearly written with an eye to a community of Christians of Jewish descent, as Mark's and Luke's gospels are written with an eye to Christians whose origins are in the Gentile world. This leads each of them to emphasise some elements of the tradition over others because those elements are important for their intended hearers and readers. A simple example of this is that Mark regularly explains Jewish customs in his gospel whereas Matthew does not because his audience is already familiar with them.

Such developments in the handing on of the gospel are not accidental; they are part and parcel of the very nature of Christianity. They go back to the reality that Jesus became a real human being,

---

[40] *Catechism of the Catholic Church*, no 126, part 3.

a Jew of the first century, living in the land of Palestine. He shared the culture, the religion and the presuppositions of his people. He 'increased in wisdom, in stature, and in divine and human favour' (Luke 2:52) within that people and culture.

As the historical journey of the Christian faith continues, a dialogue is constantly being set up between the gospel and the new cultures within which the Christian faith is being lived. It is this principle that excludes a fundamentalist approach to the Scriptures. Fundamentalism ignores the fact that the Scriptures were written in a particular context and that that context needs to be taken into account not only in their formal interpretation but in their spiritual use.

This dialogue occurring in so many new contexts is a consequence of one of the basic understandings embedded in the whole biblical tradition which is expressed in the word 'covenant'. We speak of the first covenant made through Moses and of the new covenant made in and through Jesus Christ.

A covenant is not a one-sided affair but involves a relationship between those who are in covenant with each other. The biblical covenant is between God and his people; it involves a real and reciprocal relationship between them in both the Old Testament and the New. God does not impose his word but seeks a free response from his people.

Listening to/reading the Scriptures

The texts of the gospels are crucially important to those who follow Jesus Christ. In them we have handed down to us actions and words by which we can come to discern his pattern of life, his attitudes and his general approach to the meaning of human life. In the gospels and other New Testament writings, we can see what his first followers grasped about him and the meaning of Christianity as those first generations worked that out. Our dialogue with them is constitutive of our own being followers of Jesus.

What we have seen above about the nature of the Scriptures has its consequences for our liturgical and prayerful use of them. The Scriptures are not a text book or a theological tract nor are they a catechism or a treatise on morality. They are written accounts of what happened to people who were in relationship with the revealing God. They are a means by which God continues to reveal himself in the present through the action of the Holy Spirit.

The truly 'biblical' use of the Scriptures fits into what we have said above about the covenant between God and human beings which was the context within which the Scriptures were written. The Scriptures are a means by which that covenant continues to be formed. They are a means of dialogue between God and human beings. The reality of this dialogue depends on our knowing how to use them.

Listening to the Scriptures or prayerfully reading them is not just about listening to the words which come from God. It is also about the real reaction which occurs within those who hear or read those words. Attending to the real reaction which occurs within the listener or reader is crucial. When we hear or read a passage of the Scriptures, what is our real response to it? What does it stir up in us?

There are no pre-set or necessary reactions to scriptural passages. There is nothing that we must feel or think. What is important is what we do actually feel or think. What is our real inner response? It may be delight or enlightenment or a sense of consolation but it might also be disagreement, distaste, non-understanding, puzzlement or wondering. At times, scriptural passages may make no sense to us!

It is this interplay between ourselves and the Scriptures which is crucial. What do these words do inside me? What do they stir in heart and mind? These honest inner reactions provide starting points for a dialogue between those words of the Scriptures and those who are listening to them or reading them. And in the ultimate analysis this turns out to be a dialogue between God and ourselves. This is the way in which the Scriptures can become the two-edged sword about which the Letter to the Hebrews speaks.[41] The sword that cuts into us.

In the use of the Scriptures, the covenant continues to be renewed in contemporary believers, that relationship between God and his people continues to take root and to flourish.

As we read or listen to passages of the Scriptures, we step into the shoes of the people who are in contact with Christ or God in that passage. We put ourselves in their position before the Lord and then we see what happens between us and the Lord in parallel to what happens between that person or persons and the Lord.

In that process, there will be things that do not apply to us and others which do. This is so because the person before the Lord in that passage is in a different context to ourselves and because there will be things which apply to them that do not apply to us and because there will be things that they take for granted that we do not. This will be particularly so in many Old Testament passages because the coming of Jesus the Messiah has taken us beyond the relationship to God portrayed in them into a new relationship with God grounded in Jesus the Christ.

One of the capital points in all of this is that the Scriptures are never mere texts of the past but are always seeking to find their way into us in the present.

A crucial aspect of Christian faith is embedded in this approach to the Scriptures and that is that our relationship to God is not a one-sided matter. We are not merely passively accepting God's word but are actively taking it in and letting it form a relationship with God within us. We are not fundamentalists or literalists; rather we are a people honoured by God by being taken up into a relationship with him.

Mary, the mother of Jesus, is a model in this listening to the word. If we look at the account of the Annunciation of the birth of Jesus (Luke 1:26-38), Mary's reception of the word from God is not

---

[41] Hebrews 4:12.

that of merely saying 'yes'. She goes through a process of listening and responding. First, Luke notes that she is deeply disturbed by Gabriel's words (v. 29a), secondly, she wonders what they could mean (v. 29b). Thirdly, Mary puts her finger on the great difficulty saying, "But how can this be, since I am a virgin?" (v. 34). It is at the end of this process of listening and wondering that she gives her response to the word from God: "Here I am, the Lord's servant, let it happen to me as you have said" (v. 38).

Listening to the word involved Mary herself and her questions and concerns, so it is also with us. We listen to the word and ponder and question what it might mean.

Chapter Seven

FAITHFUL TO THE FELLOWSHIP

The second element of Christian life to which the Acts of the Apostles 2:42 urges those first Christians to be faithful is the fellowship, that is the community of faith which, from earliest times, has been called the Church. Belonging to the Church, the community of faith, is an integral part of being Christian.[42] As those first Christians were called to that fidelity, so are Christians of all times.

This specific call to fidelity is a call to belong to a concrete community of faith which is made up of real human beings who have been brought together around the person of Jesus Christ and are called to follow him. In the New Testament, we can already see the evidence of that call as we can also see the concretely human and fallible character of those called to be Christ's followers. The New Testament already testifies to misunderstandings, disturbances, conflicts and real sinfulness among those first Christians.[43]

As history shows, the fact that the Church is made up of everyday human beings in all their goodness and their fallibility has been the source of great good and of many difficulties and

---

[42] The word 'Church' is commonly used today to indicate the hierarchy of the Church. The word originally meant the whole People of God, that is those who were called aside to belong to God in a new way within the human race, see for example, Exodus 19.4-6a and in the New Testament, 1 Peter 2:9-10.

[43] For example, see Mark 3:31-33, 9:33-37, 10:35-40; Matthew 16:21-23, 18:1-5, 20:20-23; Luke 9:22, 46-48; Acts 5:1-11; 1 Corinthians 5:1-13, 11:17-22.

deficiencies in the life of the Church. In our days, belonging to the Church is a problem and an obstacle for many people.[44]

It is clear that, from the very beginning of Christianity, the people involved in the Church were real human beings bearing within themselves all the things that are part of being human in all the extraordinary variety, diversity and ambiguity which that involves. The Church is a group of real human beings who are called together around Jesus Christ to live their lives as real human beings in the midst of other real human beings. Christians are not taken out of or removed from the human race but are called to belong to it in a new way. Christians were not an ideal group of human beings either in their origins or at any time in their history.[45]

This specific call for fidelity to the fellowship is a call to belong to this fallible community of believing human beings gathered around Jesus Christ. This call to be faithful to the fellowship of believers, the Church, requires a particular conversion of mind and heart in its members – a conversion to the recognition of their own common sinfulness and common need for Christ as their saviour.

At the deepest level, being faithful to this very human Church is about being faithful to humanity in its struggle to be true to itself! We cannot remove the present incompleteness or fallibility from our humanity and so we cannot simply remove those same realities from the life of the Church. The recognition of this fallibility requires that we be always alert to the 'sinfulness' which is present in the Church which is in turn a reflection of the sinfulness which is part of humanity. The Church needs to be constantly aware of and to

---

[44] A useful reference on this issue is Brian P. Flanagan, *Stumbling in Holiness. Sin and Sanctity in the Church*. Collegeville, Md.: Liturgical Press Academic, 2018.

[45] We have to be very wary of idealism; it can so easily lead us astray and – as history shows – can easily lead to violent attempts to impose the perfect society which not only does not exist but cannot exist in our present state of being. We can find such an idealist attitude in people such as some of those involved in the medieval Inquisition.

celebrate Christ's call for conversion, and also to be on the watch for the need for renewal and reform in the Church itself.

This fidelity to the Church and to humanity is inspired by and is a response to the God who is ever faithful to both. In Christ, we have God's 'yes' to the human race (2 Corinthians 1:19-20). God's fidelity to the Church is a sign of God's fidelity to all of humankind.

Humanity and this fellowship of the Church

The Church is a group of human beings taken aside by God's call to have a particular task within humanity. Let it be said again that the Church is not a group removed from humanity, but is an integral part of God's plan for humanity. This is a critical point in understanding the Church and its specific role in God's purpose for all of humankind.[46]

The original Hebrew word used to describe the People of God of the Old Testament was the word 'qahal'. This word referred to those whom God gathered to himself, the group he called from the midst of humanity to belong to him in an explicit and more intense way. The Greek of the New Testament used the word 'ekklesia' to translate 'qahal' and, in turn, English uses the word 'church' to translate that Greek word. This is the word used for the Christian communities of the New Testament.

This chosen group of people has had revealed to it and has experienced a new relationship with God. In the Scriptures, the word covenant is used to name this relationship. And the image of faithful marriage was used to describe this covenant.

---

[46] This brings up the issue of 'sect' and 'church', famously written about by the sociologist Max Weber. He makes the point in the following quotation: "Sociologically, the Church differs from the sect by considering itself the trustee of a 'trust fund' of eternal blessings that are offered to everyone" (Max Weber, *Economy and Society: An Outline of Interpretive Sociology*, [edited by Guenther Roth & Claus Witch]. Berkeley, Los Angeles, London: University of California Press, 1978, p. 1164.

There have been two stages to this covenant – the first is the covenant made through Moses which is recorded in the books of the Old Testament and the second is the covenant made in and through Jesus the Christ which is recorded in the books of the New Testament, and which is the new and eternal relationship between God and human beings. In it is expressed the unending fidelity of God. This covenant begins and continues on God's initiative.

The core of this relationship between God and the chosen People was expressed in terms of God speaking his word to them through chosen figures. In the new covenant, that word becomes an actual human being in the person of Jesus Christ. He is God's self-expression in his very person. He is God's self-expression in human flesh as we discussed in the last chapter.

The People of God finds its very nature and purpose in its having an 'in-between' character. This people is described as a "priestly, prophetic and kingly people".[47] To make sense of such a phrase, we need to see this group, the Church, in its essential relationship to all of humankind. It does not exist for its own sake, but as a sign and an instrument[48] of God's plan for all of humankind. This relationship to all of humanity is crucial for an understanding of the nature of the Church.

The new era in which we are living puts to the Church the question of its own identity. In the contemporary situation, a Church centred on itself loses credibility and cannot be seen to reflect the gospel it proclaims. Its relationship to humanity is constitutive of its nature. It is a bridge between God as revealed in Jesus Christ and God's plan for all human beings. This takes us well beyond the vision of the Church expressed in the once common

---

[47] 1 Peter 2:4-10 (Exodus 19:5-6). Vatican II, *Constitution on the Church (Lumen Gentium)*, 9-17 (This document henceforth referred to as L.G.). Also see the *Roman Missal*, First Preface for Sundays in Ordinary Time.

[48] L.G. 1

adage: "Outside the Church, no salvation" which expresses an understanding of the Church which has been formally set aside.[49]

The first Preface for Sundays in the Roman Missal describes the gathered community as "a chosen race, a royal priesthood, a holy nation, a people for your own possession (i.e. God's possession) to proclaim everywhere your mighty works, for you have called us out of darkness into your own wonderful light".

This group is to be priestly, that is they are to come before the Father in the name of all humankind. When they are at Eucharist, they are at the centre of innumerable loosely scattered concentric circles stretching to the ends of the universe. As the Fourth Eucharistic Prayer in the Roman Missal prays: "Remember those who take part in this offering, those here present and all your people, and all who seek you with a sincere heart", and "Remember those who have died in the peace of Christ and all the dead whose faith is known to you alone".

This people is prophetic – that is, they have heard the word of God in Christ and have had a glimpse of what the Father is preparing for all humankind in his promised future. They are to witness to God's vision and purpose for all God's creation and to trace out in themselves the way of life which leads to it.

They are a kingly people in terms of Christ's kingship of service, a kingship whose throne is the cross, on which he is given for all humankind. It is a 'kingship' of self-giving service to a human race in its journey to the One who is Father and Mother of all.

'Sacrament'

In the documents of the Second Vatican Council, the Church is presented as the sign and instrument of God's purpose in bringing

---

[49] For a thorough treatment of the adage 'Outside the Church, no salvation', see F. A. Sullivan, *Salvation outside the Church? Tracing the History of the Catholic Response*. N.Y/Mahwah: Paulist Press, 1992.

humankind into unity with himself and each other. The Church is thus described as being 'in the nature of a sacrament' of communion with God and of unity among all human beings.[50]

What this indicates is that what God has revealed of himself and his plans in the life of the People of God is an image of and an instrument for what God is seeking to bring about in all of humankind. This reconciliation of all with each other and with the One who gives life to all is the form that the salvation of the world is seeking to take. It involves the overcoming of the separation and alienation which constantly afflict our human world and which keeps it separated from God.

We may compare God's working in the Church and God's working in his world to an iceberg. A part of an iceberg appears above the waters but by far the greater part of it exists under the waters. The Church is like that part of the iceberg which is above the waters and is visible; and we may compare God's working in his whole world to that greater part of the iceberg which is below the waters and is not visible; but the visible and the invisible parts belong to the same iceberg. But we can only recognise the submerged part of the iceberg because we can see the part which appears above the waters.

So it is with the Church and God's activity in his whole world. In the Church we have a fragile image of what God is at work seeking to bring about in all of humankind. The universal activity of God has been explicitly revealed in the image and instrument of that activity which is the community of believers in Jesus Christ, that is the Church. The Church is that universal activity of God in miniature.

'First fruits'

An image which the New Testament uses to relate Christians to the rest of humankind is that of the 'first fruits'. This image is based in the Old Testament. It is a religious image with an agricultural background.

---

[50] L.G. 1.

The first fruits were the first part of the crop to be harvested. They were reaped and given over to God in recognition of and thanksgiving for the whole harvest, all which was God's gift. The first fruits are the first part of the whole harvest; they belong to the whole harvest and they represent the whole harvest and find their meaning in the whole. So it is with the Church; it is that part of humankind which has already discovered God in Christ but they do this as part of the whole of humanity and as representing the whole of humankind.

St Paul uses this image in referring to Epaenetus as the first fruits of Asia to Christ (Romans 16:5) and to Stephanus' family as the first fruits of Achaia (1 Corinthians 16:15). That is, they have come to Christ as the first of their people and the first fruits of Christ's harvest among all their people.

The Church finds its proper identity in this image indicating its relationship to the whole of humankind; the Church makes no sense without its belonging to the whole. The Church is about what is beyond itself; it is about what God is doing beyond itself. It is the servant of the God who will gather the whole harvest to himself. God seeks to gather all of humankind into his home, into his kingdom and to his table.[51]

---

[51] As with the whole Christian mystery, the understanding of the Church is unfolded as it moves on through the various stages of its history. In each age, new questions and perspectives arise which make believers look again at the nature of the Church and at what these perspectives might unearth of its relationship to Christ and his work. The idea of a specific theology of the Church (ecclesiology) is a recent theme in understanding the faith. The Church was simply taken for granted for most of Christian history and no need was felt to explain it or elaborate its meaning. The Reformation changed that attitude as its denials required in response a justification of the nature of the Church as understood in Catholicism. Then in the last hundred years or so, studies of the New Testament and the writings of the Fathers of the Church brought to light a deeper and more theological understanding of the nature of the Church. This is reflected in the profound presentation of the Church in the documents of the Second Vatican Council and in particular in its Constitution on the Church (*Lumen Gentium*) and the Constitution on the Church in the Contemporary World (*Gaudium et Spes*).

It is 'We' who pray

In the Eucharist, all of the prayer is in the first-person plural, that is, it is always 'We" who are praying even when the prayer is being expressed by the priest. The priest's prayer in the Eucharist is never his individual prayer but always that of the whole community of faith.

In the light of the understanding of the Church outlined above, that 'We' can be extended to the whole of humankind, which is symbolised in the community gathered explicitly around Jesus Christ. In the first instance, the 'We" of prayer applies to the gathered Church but seeing the Church as the first fruits of all humanity and of creation symbolically extends that 'We' to the whole of humankind and indeed to all of creation.

In this perspective, the Church is turned towards humankind in all their common joys and hopes, their griefs and anxieties. In this spirit, the Church finds resounding in itself everything that is genuinely human, being itself a cell of that humankind.[52] A Church which sees itself as separated from the world cannot fulfil its God-given role.

The Church belongs to Christ

Early on in this chapter, the Church was described as a group of real human beings who have been brought together around Jesus Christ. It is Jesus Christ who gives this group its identity, its meaning and its mission.

In the Scriptures, God is often given the name of those people whose God he is. So we find God named as 'the God of Abraham', 'the God of Jacob', 'the God of Moses', 'the God of Israel'. In such naming, God is understood by reference to those whom God has called. God is tied to those people to whom he has in some way

---

[52] G.& S. 1.

made himself known. God is implicated with them and one might even say that God is at their mercy. For good and for ill, they are like the 'face' of God to others around them.

The revelation of God in the New Testament is tied in with the person of Jesus Christ; God is the 'God and Father of our Lord Jesus Christ'. God is the 'Abba' of Jesus. And this flows on into the Church. The Church is radically tied to the person of Jesus the Christ; it has no significance or purpose without him.

This finds expression in some powerful images in the New Testament whose purpose is to help us see into the depth of the communion which exists between Jesus and the community of his disciples.

St Paul uses the image of the Church as the body of Christ (Romans 6:1; 12:3-12; 1 Corinthians 10:16-17; 11:29; 12:1-31; Ephesians 1:15-23; 4:1-6; Colossians 3:12-17). This image has become the most common image of the Church's union with Christ in the Christian tradition. In some of Paul's texts, the Church is compared to a human body which lives with the life of the person which infuses it and then in other texts, Christ is seen as the head and the Church as the body belonging to the head. In both cases, this body is made up of many functioning parts, all of which have their particular purpose within the unity of the whole.

This goes beyond the idea that the Church is a body in the sense that we can speak of a group of people as a social body. It implies a sharing of life between Christ and his disciples; a sharing of life which is brought about in the sharing of the life-giving bread and wine of the Eucharist.

In John's gospel, the relationship between Christ and his disciples is described as a mutual indwelling (John 14:23-31; 17:20-23) and in terms of the image of the vine and the branches (John 15:1-17) in which Christ is the whole vine and his disciples the branches. In the first letter of Peter (2:4-10), the image that is used is that of a spiritual temple of which Christians are the living stones. All of these images are images of living union.

A structured community of faith

Every human community has structures. If such structures do not come about in some recognised way, they tend to arise informally.

From the time of the gospels, there were leaders in the community of faith. The first formal leaders were the apostles who were also referred to as the Twelve. The number twelve is significant in that it symbolises the gathering of the new People of God. As there were the twelve patriarchs and the twelve tribes of the People of God of the Old Testament, so there were to be the Twelve apostles as the leaders of the People of God of the New Testament.

New structures of leadership began to emerge in the churches founded by the apostles and by other early Christian leaders. In the New Testament, these ministries are presented as being quite fluid. There is mention of bishops, presbyters and deacons along with other ministries but there does not seem to be any great consistency in the form which those ministries took at that stage of the Church's history.

It was in the first half of the second century that such roles began to become organised into the structures which have been passed down through the centuries to our own day. These structures have seen many modifications along the way. In these structures, the bishop is the presiding leader of the Church with a group of elders (presbyters) around him and deacons who were ministers to the bishop especially in the practicalities of the life of the Church: care for those in need and in administration. These ministries found expression in corresponding liturgical roles.

As the life of the Church developed and became more complex, the presbyters came to be delegated by the bishop to preside at liturgical celebrations separate from his own. And as the Church expanded, such presbyters became leaders of separate communities within the bishop's diocese and pastoral care. These communities were parallel to what we would call 'parishes' today and their presiding ministers parallel to those whom we would call 'priests' today.

From New Testament times, all the individual churches were seen as in communion with each other. The Church was not only local but also universal and structures developed to express its universal nature. Bishops gathered in local synods or councils to resolve difficult matters and in universal or Ecumenical Councils when very significant matters arose. These councils were an initial expression of collegiality which describes the universal body of bishops which has a responsibility for the wellbeing of all the Church. The bishop of Rome, the Pope, is the leader of the College of Bishops and, as such, has a primacy in the whole Church.

These structures have undergone considerable historical reshaping. Pope Francis is putting into effect an understanding of the Church which is both ancient and appropriate to our times. This goes by the name of Synodality. This word from its Greek roots means 'being on the way together'. Synodality is based on the nature of the Church as a functioning whole, that is as a communion of life and faith among all the faithful, whatever their ministry might be. It seeks to promote the back-and-forth communication between all the members of the Church.

Pope Francis is promoting Synodality both as an expression of the nature of the Church and as a method with which to move into the future unitedly. Synodality is about mutual listening and the discernment of the voice of the Holy Spirit emerging in the whole Church. It asks everyone to bracket their own point of view and to listen to what others have to say. It involves discerning what the Spirit is saying to the Church in the concrete situation of the time. It involves reading the signs of the times in the light of the gospel.

Synodality is a new word for most Catholics but it takes the nature of the Church as a communion seriously and is a genuine development of the understanding of the Church which emerged at Vatican II. And it offers a precious way into the future which emphasises unity and mutual listening and respect. Is it a means by which God is opening a way ahead before his people?

Chapter Eight

FAITHFUL TO THE BREAKING OF THE BREAD

The third element of the Christian faith to which Christians are called to be faithful is the breaking of the bread (Acts 2:42). This term – the breaking of the bread – is used by St Luke to describe the Lord's Supper or what we call the Eucharist both in his gospel (24:13-35) and the Acts of the Apostles (2:42, 46; 20:7).

The Breaking of the Bread lies at the very heart of the life of those who follow Jesus Christ. The words of Jesus recorded in the New Testament 'Do this in memory of me' make this action something which Christians cannot ignore.[53]

This action has its spiritual and ritual roots in the Old Testament and especially in the sacred meals of Judaism. The Eucharist fundamentally differs from those meals in that it finds its specific character in its reference to the death and resurrection of Jesus which the New Testament sees as fulfilling the expectation of the coming of the Messiah in the Old Testament.

The breaking of the bread

The Passover meal – as with other Jewish holy meals – began with the breaking of the bread, that is the breaking of the one loaf into

---

[53] Luke 22:19; 1 Corinthians 11:23-27. This phrase is included in the Narrative of Institution (Consecration) in all the Eucharistic Prayers.

as many pieces as there were people taking part in the meal. This action established the unity of the group by their sharing that one loaf. They all drew life from the One who is the source of life in the sharing of that one loaf of bread. That loaf of bread came to them from the life-giving Creator and so this breaking and sharing was an acknowledgment of and a thanksgiving to the creating God. This was made clear in the prayers that accompanied the action of the bread-breaking. This Jewish ritual became the matrix of the Christian sacred meal and its name became one of the names of the Christ-centred meal of Christianity.

In his First Letter to the Corinthians, St Paul expresses clearly the meaning of the breaking of the bread: "...and the loaf of bread which we break, is it not a sharing in the body of Christ? As there is one loaf, so we, although there are many of us, are one single body, for we all share in the one loaf" (10:16-17). In that passage, we have what is probably the earliest explicit New Testament reference to the Eucharist.

Fidelity to the breaking of the bread is tied into fidelity to the fellowship presented in the last chapter. This fellowship, this communion, is established in the breaking of the bread as we saw was also the case with its Jewish antecedent.

So we get an interplay in the action of the breaking of the bread between that action and the group doing that action; the group entering into that action is drawn into communion with each other and with the life-giving God. The Christian breaking of the bread was accompanied by the words of Jesus over the bread and cup of wine – my body given for you, my blood shed for you. In those words, that bread and wine is drawn together with his death the next day.

Later, this interplay between the action of breaking the bread and the group doing the action will be developed by the Fathers of the Church in the phrase "the Church 'makes' the Eucharist and the Eucharist 'makes' the Church". That is, the Church in celebrating the Eucharist becomes what it is, a communion in the death and resurrection of Jesus Christ.

This is a basis for the centrality of the Sunday Eucharist. It puts the Sunday gathering of the Church at the forefront of Christian life and it differentiates the Sunday Eucharist from all other celebrations of the Eucharist. All members of the Church are called to gather for the Sunday Eucharist since it is there that the Church becomes the Church whose life-giving core is communion with the risen Lord.[54] Other celebrations of the Eucharist are valuable but they do not have the same significance as the Sunday Eucharist because the whole community of faith is not called to gather for them.

Paul sees this 'communion' in the one loaf as a communion in the body of Christ given for us just as he sees the sharing of the one cup as a sharing in the blood of Christ shed for us (1 Corinthians 10:15). In the same letter to the Corinthians, Paul gives us an account of what Jesus did at the Last Supper (1 Corinthians 11:23-27), which echoes the accounts given in the gospels of Mark, Matthew and Luke. Each of these accounts have differing and enlightening details to them (Mark 14:22-25; Matthew 26:26-29; Luke 22:15-20), but they clearly refer to the same central event in the life of Jesus.

Each of the gospel accounts presents the words and actions of Jesus as constituting a part of the overall account of his suffering and death. Similarly, in Paul's account, Jesus' action is situated 'on the night he was betrayed', linking Last Supper and his death.

The actions and words of Jesus at the Supper are stretched towards his death; they point to and interpret his death. As Paul says: "As often as you eat this bread and drink this cup, you are proclaiming the Lord's death until he comes" (1 Corinthians 11:26). In the words and actions of Jesus, the bread and the cup of wine coalesce with his death to which he is consecrating himself at the Supper.

The bread and wine of the Eucharist are our means of communion with his death, whose other face is the resurrection.

---

[54] This found expression in later times in attendance at Sunday Mass becoming a law of the Church and in some situations a civil law.

The living risen Lord draws us into communion with himself and the life he now lives beyond death. In the Eucharist, human beings are already passing over through life-doomed-to-death into life beyond the power of death.

Do this in memory of me

To understand the Eucharist, it is important to give weight to the New Testament phrase 'Do this in memory of me'. At times, the word memory has mistakenly been taken to mean a mere mental recalling of the death and resurrection of Jesus. Biblically, however, the word 'memorial' has a much deeper meaning.[55]

For the Scriptures, remembering is about taking stock of the reality that one's roots are deeply sunk in past events whose effects continue in the present. So memorial is remembering events or persons who gave origin to what continues to exist.

In Israel, this applied especially to the Exodus out of Egypt and the journey of their ancestors through the desert into the promised land. This was the event to which Israel traced its origins and which was at the source of its continuing existence. The continuing result of the Exodus was the promised land in which the people of Israel dwelt and found their livelihood and their freedom.

That land fed them; it kept them alive. Their possession of the land was symbolised in their liturgy by the fruits which that land produced to give them life – so in their liturgy they used the bread and wine grown in that land as the symbols of that land. These were the concrete evidence of their possession of the land and these foods were, therefore, the continuing fruits of the Exodus. This accounts for the use of bread and wine – among other things – in the Passover celebration. The Exodus was an event of the past which stretched

---

[55] A profound presentation of the meaning of memorial can be found in Brevard Childs, *Memory and Tradition in Israel*. London: SCM Press,1962. See also Frank O'Loughlin, *The Eucharist: Doing What Jesus Did*. Strathfield, NSW: St Pauls Publications,1997, pp. 35-62.

into the present in the fruits of the land which the people enjoyed in their present time.

If we think about this understanding of memorial, we can see that it is still at work among us in many of our human celebrations. When we celebrate a birthday, we are celebrating the person who is alive among us and significant to us, and we celebrate that person by reference to their birth, that is their origin. It is the same in the celebration of anniversaries of any kind. Even in celebrating the anniversary of someone who has died, we are celebrating the importance of that person and the poignant state in which death left those who loved them. We 'celebrate' their absence and the gap that that absence leaves in the lives of those around them.

This principle is also at work in public celebrations such as national days like Anzac Day and Australia Day. The controversy surrounding the date of Australia Day illustrates the same principle. This controversy calls into question the role of European settlement as being at the origins of Australia which was the presumption behind the celebration in previous times. This ignored the reality of Australia as it existed before European settlement took place. In all of this, the question of the identity of the nation is brought to the fore. The things of which we celebrate the memory establish who we are, and, if their importance is called into question, there usually follows considerable conflict.

★★★

In line with the biblical tradition of memory, when we celebrate the Eucharist, we do so in memory of the death and resurrection of Jesus.[56] The death of Jesus issued in his resurrection, that is in the life he came into, in and through his death. So in the Eucharist, we are remembering or making memorial of someone who is alive. Thus the Eucharistic memorial essentially involves the presence of

---

[56] This is stated in each Eucharistic Prayer immediately after the Narrative of Institution, in that part of the Eucharistic Prayer called the Memorial or the Anamnesis.

the risen Jesus. In the case of the Eucharistic memorial, the presence of the risen Jesus and our sharing of his risen life arises from the nature of the event of which we make memorial – Christ's death into resurrection. The continuing presence of the risen Jesus is at the heart of the Eucharist.

The Eucharist does not involve another form of the presence of Christ or another location of that presence. It is the presence of the Lord in his risen state drawing us into communion with himself. The presence of Christ in the Eucharist is not an addition to the mystery of his death and resurrection but a part of it, a dimension of it, an extension of it into his gathered people through the bread they break and eat and the wine they drink.

It is the memorial of his death and resurrection into which we are being drawn by eating that bread and drinking that cup. We are indeed eating and drinking, that is we are taking life-giving elements into ourselves, we are being nourished on the risen life of Jesus. He is feeding that life into us in parallel to the way ordinary bread and wine feed our present life into us. He is giving us authentic life-giving bread and wine which is giving to us and promising us life beyond the power of death.

Becoming the Body of Christ

In the Eucharist, we are being drawn into such a communion with Christ that St Paul used the image of the body of Christ to describe the Church. St Paul says, as we saw above: "The cup of blessing which we bless, is it not fellowship in the blood of Christ? The bread which we break, is it not a fellowship in the body of Christ? As there is one bread, so we, though many, are one body; for we all share in the one bread" (1 Corinthians 10:16-17). St Augustine makes this same point graphically by saying that, as we celebrate the Eucharist, we become what we eat![57] That is, we take this communion with Christ into us. We become a communion of life with Christ. And it is primarily a matter of 'We' and not merely 'I'. The communion with Christ is indeed personal but not individual; it is communion with each other in and through our communion with Christ.

Doing what he did

At the Sunday Eucharist, the gathered People of God do what Jesus did in memory of him. It is the action of the whole community within which the priest or bishop has the pivotal role of doing the specific actions and saying the specific words that Jesus did and said as we have them in the gospel accounts of the Last Supper and in Paul's First Letter to the Corinthians.[58] The whole community does this action in which, as Yves Congar says, the Holy Spirit concelebrates with us.[59] The action of the Eucharist is served by the ministry of the priest whose service or ministry it is to stimulate and lead the whole community in its entering into communion with Christ, that is in its becoming the body of Christ.

Having heard and been nourished at the table of the word of God, the People of God enter into the action of the Eucharist. They do what Jesus did at the Last Supper: bread and wine is taken to the altar (the presentation of gifts), God is given thanks and praise (the Eucharistic Prayer), the bread is broken (the breaking of the bread), bread and wine is given to be received (communion). The whole structure of the Liturgy of the Eucharist is based on the actions of Christ at the Last Supper at which he took bread and wine, gave

---

[57] Sermon 272. For easy reference, see Daniel J Sheerin, *The Eucharist. Message of the Fathers of the Church 7*. Wilmington, Delaware: Michael Glazier, 1986, 95.
[58] Mark 14:22-24; Matthew 26:26-28; Luke 22:19-20; 1 Corinthians 11:23-25.
[59] "The Holy Spirit concelebrates with us in order to make Christ's work a reality here and now" Yves Congar, *The Word and the Spirit*. London/San Francisco: Geoffrey Chapman/ Harper and Row publishers, 1986, p. 35.

God thanks and praise over them, broke the bread and gave the bread and cup to his disciples.

There is also a deeper sense to our doing what Jesus did. In his action at the Last Supper, Jesus hands over his life to what is to come about in his death the next day and in so doing he is entrusting himself utterly into the Father's hands.

In celebrating the Eucharist, we are drawn into Jesus' handing over of himself into the Father's hands. Jesus does that in the face of his death and we are drawn into that same handing over of ourselves in the course of whatever life presents us with in our present circumstances, in time to come and ultimately in the face of our own deaths.

This aspect of the Eucharist has often been described as a sacrifice. This is an acceptable description so long as our thinking about it arises out of the Scriptures. For the biblical tradition, sacrifices were the means given by God to enable his people to enter into communion with him. They were seen as his gift to them. They were the God-given means by which Israel could enter into communion with God. This needs to shape any use we make of this term.

Jesus fulfils that biblical tradition. However, he comes from God not to offer a ritual sacrifice but to live a human life. He is God's gift to us to create a new communion between God and human beings. He does this by living out a human life in total communion with the Father in the concrete circumstances of his life, work and times. This culminates in his death and resurrection by which he passes over into the fullness of communion with God. This communion with God – which is the source of all holiness – is given to us as we are drawn into communion with his death and resurrection. And the fact that this is our ultimate destiny may mean that we are called to give up other things in order to come into that communion. This finds expression in the everyday meaning of sacrifice as the giving up of something for the sake of something more important.

The Mass: a problem?

Given what has been said above, I can hear some people saying that they cannot recognise any of it in the celebrations of the Mass of which they have been a part. This touches on a real problem. And it is, I believe, an element of the transition through which we are passing and of the different places on the spectrum of feeling and thinking on which members of the Church find themselves at the present time. There are many attitudes and feelings about the Mass among the People of God and, significantly also, among priests.

In some situations, the Mass is celebrated as if the reforms of Vatican II had never happened, not only among those who do not go along with the reforms but also among those who have accepted what is new in the rites and prayers but continue to celebrate in the spirit and mood of the previous liturgy.

There are those people who continue to go to Mass with the primary intention of fulfilling their Sunday obligation. This is sincerely a part of their faith as they have grown up in it. For many other people, this is simply not enough; they are looking for deeper involvement and explicit recognition of their place and role within the liturgy and the Church. For them, it is simply not enough to be at Mass; rather, Mass is something they are there to do and be involved in. They are not happy to be passively present at something which the priest does and into which they cannot find a satisfying point of entry. At times they find that their pastors are impervious to the problems they are experiencing.

A great part of the response to this problem lies in the hands of priests whose role in the liturgy is central. In the pre-Vatican II liturgy, the role of priests was dominant, in fact the Mass was seen as really being their business and the People were basically seen as attendees. Such is no longer the case as the principles of the reformed liturgy make clear.[60]

---

[60] To follow up on this, see my earlier book *Gather the People of God*. Bayswater, Vic: Coventry Press, 2020.

There is often still a presumption at work in the celebration of the liturgy that the liturgy works in the sort of supernaturalist fashion which means that involvement and participation of the people does not ultimately matter. However, for its fruitfulness, the liturgy requires the interplay of the Mystery being celebrated and the positive openness and involvement of those participating in it.

As has been repeated several times in the course of this work, the People of God are involved in a covenant with the Lord and this is a two-way process and it is played out in the liturgy. As also mentioned several times earlier in this book, the involvement and participation of the people becomes more crucial when external social supports of faith are no longer present and effective. In this new situation, the interior supports for growth in faith and Christian identity become determinative.

There is a great need for deeper formation in the liturgy for both for the whole People of God and for the clergy as is suggested in Pope Francis' recent Apostolic Letter *Desiderio desideravi* on liturgical formation.

Seven sacraments

In the Catholic tradition, there are the other six sacraments which are clustered around the Eucharist. They form an organic unity leading to the Eucharist or extending its reach and significance.

Baptism and Confirmation

Baptism and Confirmation initiate the Christian into the Eucharist in which the community of faith is established and is given its identity in communion with Christ. This relationship was very clear in the ancient practice in which the person was baptised, then confirmed by the bishop and was then taken into the Eucharistic community – all done in the one liturgy usually at the Easter Vigil. These three sacraments being celebrated together is still the practice in the Eastern churches, even for infants, with the presbyter presiding over all three rites of initiation.

In the Western Church, once infant baptism became the norm, baptism became separated from confirmation (reserved to the bishop) which was celebrated later if at all! As a result of this practice, it came about that people were brought to the Eucharist before they were confirmed. This has caused quite some confusion in the interrelatedness of these sacraments. And as is often said, it made of confirmation a sacrament looking for its true meaning and place in the Christian life.

Penance

The sacrament of penance has a history of great variety. But it began as a second form of baptism for those who had sinned in such a way as to put their Christian identity in doubt and so could not celebrate the Eucharist. In its earliest form, it was a very ecclesial celebration which culminated in the penitent's readmission to the Eucharist. In the course of its history, the sacrament took forms which were much more concerned with the individual.

Anointing of the Sick

Anointing of the Sick is the sacrament which extends the healing ministry of the Lord into the time of the Church. The sacrament is not about physical healing but about that deeper healing arising from the death and resurrection of the Lord which is celebrated in the Eucharist. What is given in this sacrament of the sick are the fruits of the Spirit of the Risen Lord: peace, serenity, sure and certain hope and perseverance. These gifts are the presence in the sick person of the influence of the Lord's resurrection. In one of the earliest documents we have, the anointed sick are seen – by their very anointing – as exercising the priestly, prophetic and servant role of the People of God.[61] This is a dimension of the sacrament worth emphasising again. It is an application of what we celebrate in the Eucharist.

Marriage

The sacrament of Marriage celebrates the union of Christ and his people which is brought about in the Eucharist. This paralleling of the married couple and the relationship of Christ and his people is often presented very idealistically, so much so that it can sound unreal.

But the relationship of Christ and his people is something forged in the everyday life of those who follow Christ. It requires a constant commitment to listen to Christ's word and let it find a home in the disciple in the course of which a union with Christ is gradually achieved. This is the process which finds an echo and an embodiment in the relationship of wife and husband. This likening of marriage to the relationship of Christ and his people is not some other-worldly reality but a matter of the everyday life of committed couples.

Orders

The sacrament of Orders, as its name implies, is about the ordering the community of faith, of giving it unity and form. Ordained ministers are ministers of communion whose ministry is concerned with unity of the Church.

Ordained ministers are ministers to the communion or what we might call 'hinge' ministers. Bishops are the leaders of the local diocesan Church and also belong to the college of bishops

---

[61] This terminology is used in the early Roman prayer for the blessing of the Oil of the Sick called by its first word: the 'Emitte' and in the document called *The Apostolic Tradition*, attributed to Hippolytus.

whose head is the bishop of Rome, the Pope. So bishops are a hinge between the universal Church and the local diocesan Church. Presbyters (priests) are leaders of the Church in their locally gathered or particular communities; they are also members of the presbyterium or college of priests whose head is the bishop. Thus they are hinges between the locally gathering Church (parishes) and the diocesan Church.

In the communally structured Catholic Church, these ministers are the linking points of unity and it is they who lead the celebration of the Eucharist precisely because they are the hinges or servants of communion within the Church, which is both local and universal.

Other rituals

There are other rituals which are part of the life of the Church. The most important of these is the Christian Funeral. This is not a sacrament in itself even though it can involve the celebration of the Eucharist. It is not a sacrament because sacraments belong to the life we now live and do not belong to the life of glory which we are to inherit. And it is into this life of glory that the Christian funeral commits the dead. The funeral which celebrates the person's passover into the risen life of Christ brings all that has happened in the sacraments to their fulfilment. We celebrate the person's death by having the celebration of the Eucharist because they now share at the table of the Father's kingdom of which the Eucharist is an image and a prophecy.

Blessings of persons and things are also part of the Church's liturgical life. These blessings recognise in the good things of this world the gifts of God, that is, his blessings. In ritual blessings, we give God thanks for what he has given us and pray that he may continue to bless us in our relationships and in our use of his good gifts.

There is also the Liturgy of the Hours. This is the continuing prayer of the Church made up of a series of hours of prayer

Into the Future

throughout the day: Morning Prayer and Evening Prayer are the major hours, then there is Prayer during the day and Compline which is a night prayer designed for the very end of the day. There is also an Office of Readings which can be prayed at any time of the day. The Liturgy of the Hours is also used in monasteries in a more extended form.

There are also various devotions which make up part of the prayer life of the People of God. These are not considered part of the official prayer of the Church. They are often directed to the Lord under various titles or to the Blessed Virgin or to one or other of the saints. They have often arisen because of the absence of an appreciation of the Scriptures in the spiritual lives of Catholics, and perhaps because of the lack of real participation of the people in the spirituality and prayer of the liturgy. They provided a means of participation and devotional satisfaction for people. They often met the religious needs of the people in ways that the liturgy did not. There is a process of approval required for these devotions to assure of their consonance with the Christian faith.

Chapter Nine

FAITHFUL TO PRAYER

The fourth thing to which Christians are called to be faithful is prayer or 'the prayers' as the Acts of the Apostles puts it. Prayer is of the essence of the Christian faith and the other three things to which the passage from the Acts of the Apostles calls us are all suffused and carried forward by prayer. They cannot happen without being lived or done in a prayerful spirit.

Praying was a part of the inheritance that the Christian faith received from Judaism. The biblical prayers of the Old Testament – the psalms in particular – still remain a daily and fundamental part of Christian communal prayer in the Mass, the Liturgy of the Hours and the celebration of the sacraments. And some of these ancient prayers form part of the personal prayer of individual Christians.

The psalms remain fundamental because they encapsulate the spiritual journey lived throughout the history recorded in the old testament as it reaches out towards the coming of the Christ. The Church as a communion along with each Christian person has to live something of that same journey towards Christ in their own lives and in their own times. We can find in those Old Testament prayers images of our own individual spiritual journey and of the Church's spiritual journey as a communion of faith living in real human history.

The psalms display the whole variety of human emotions and attitudes which are expressed and lived out before God. We find everything in them: the search for and the finding of God, the questioning of God, the fear of God; we find within them human goodness, human joy and fulfilment, human fear, human hatred of those who oppose us, and human violence and that violence at times in horrific forms. All of life is there in the psalms and it is all brought to the surface before God. The psalms do not pretend; they are the prayers of real human beings in the throes of all the ups and downs that make up human life. They are not interested in unreal idealism or pretty devotions. Their realism is important for the realism, the practice and the fruitfulness of Christian prayer.

Within the above perspective, it is legitimate and fruitful to be selective in the use of the psalms. This is the case with the liturgy's use of them.[62] The psalms, like all of the Old Testament, show a development and a refinement in their understanding of God from the earlier psalms to the later.

The spirit of Christian prayer has grown out of the developing understanding of God which was emerging throughout the Old Testament. But as with all things Christian, the prayer of Christians has been radically reshaped around the person and prayer of Jesus the Christ.

Life-oriented prayer

Christian prayer is not an avoidance of the issues which confront human beings in the course of their lives. It is not a means of avoiding responsibility and action; it is not the opium of the people as Karl Marx would have it. Christian prayer immerses us in the issues of human life from a particular point of view. A point of view which sees the world coming to us from the hands of God who creates a relationship with human beings. This relationship, as has been said above, has a mutual and reciprocal dimension to it: it requires that human beings – within that relationship with God –

---

[62] The liturgy chooses certain psalms for use in the Mass and sacraments. It sometimes chooses only some verses of a psalm and there are psalms which it never uses. There is a wider use of psalms in the Liturgy of the Hours and in monastic prayer all psalms are normally used.

use the freedom and talents which come to them from the creating God.

Christian prayer is prayer which is buoyed up by faith in Christ who is God-with-us (Emmanuel). Christ reveals to us that God is with us in all that makes up our human lives. God is with us historically in the person of Christ but the risen Lord remains with us all, in all the real moments and events of our lives "for better, for worse, for richer, for poorer, in sickness and in health",[63] until death does us unite.

In prayer as in life there come to be times when we know that there is nothing more that we can do, that we have reached the end of our resources. There may be times when, with Jesus on the cross, we can only pray Psalm 21 which begins "My God, my God, why have you deserted me?" but ends in an act of trust. Such trust is also expressed in the words of Jesus on the cross in Luke's gospel: "Into your hands I commend my spirit". So it is that in all situations in life, the ultimate prayer of the Christian is to entrust into the hands of the living God their lives, themselves, those for whom they pray, and the world itself. Our prayer always has an aspect of watching and waiting to it (Psalm 5:2-10) and it seeks not the miraculous but that God may open a way before us. We only find that way ahead by the watching and waiting that is so often a part of prayer. Such an opening of a way ahead is characteristic of the whole history of God's dealings with his people as we saw earlier in this book.

Prayer is a human thing and is shaped by our own personality, stage of development and life context. In the development of prayer, the relationship between the communal prayer of the Church (the liturgy) and the personal prayer of Christians needs to be in fruitful interplay; these two dimensions of prayer feed into each other.

The document of the Second Vatican Council on the Liturgy makes the statement that the active participation of the people is "the primary and indispensable source from which the faithful are

---

[63] Marriage imagery is an integral part of the biblical understanding of God's covenant with human beings, and of Christ's relationship with his people.

to derive the true Christian spirit".[64] So Christian prayer in its whole breadth needs to be nourished by the prayer of the liturgy which includes so much of the Scriptures. But there is another aspect to this – that the personal prayer of Christians enables them to be receptive of the prayer of the liturgy and feeds into the prayer of the liturgy. There is a mutual relationship between the prayer of the Christian liturgy and the personal prayer of Christians.

Prayer today

Given the pluralist and secular society in which we live, prayer becomes even more important for the believer. In earlier formally Christian centuries, there was a social and cultural Christian scaffolding around believers supporting their faith, which has been discussed earlier in this book. This scaffolding consisted in the fact that everyone believed and so people were carried forward by the Christian structure around them, presuming it to be the natural state of things.

People became genuine believers in that situation by absorbing their faith from the social atmosphere surrounding them. However, that social scaffolding no longer exists and so there is an increased need for a building up and a reinforcement of the interior dimensions of the faith. And a crucial part of that interior support structure is prayer and its development among all those who make up the Church.

It is in prayer that the influence of Christ can take root in us, that a deep conviction about Christ and his gospel can arise within us. It is in prayer that the person of Christ can become more real to us and can turn our hearts to himself, claiming us more deeply as his own (John 13:1). This is particularly true of a type of prayer which ponders over the gospels.

---

[64] Vatican II, *Constitution on the Sacred Liturgy (Sacrosanctum Concilium)*, no. 14, paragraph 2.

As spoken about earlier, an interesting phenomenon in the secular and pluralist societies of our days is the rise of a desire for and practices of spirituality. We find many groups and individuals seeking ways in which to tap into various traditions of spirituality and meditation. There is an upsurge of interest in the traditions of Christian spirituality. And there is increased interest in Eastern traditions, in Buddhism and Hinduism in particular. People can find real value in these traditions which help in the development of spiritual attitudes and values. In a society which is in danger of dismissing the spiritual, the contribution of these movements is valuable.

From a Christian point of view, there is an inherent possibility in some of these movements that they do not go beyond the discovery of the depths of the human and of the created world or that they refer to an understanding of the transcendent which does not coincide with the mystery of God as revealed by and in Christ.

In the Christian tradition and indeed in the whole biblical tradition, prayer is understood as a dialogue between God and human beings. This, of course, rests on the biblical discovery of God as personal, that is as one who enters into relationship with human beings. This, as we have seen, is inherent in that fundamental idea of the Scriptures – the covenant between God and human beings.

In looking towards evangelisation, the desire for spirituality in our society is a starting point that calls for a response from the Church. As Christians, we have a rich tradition of prayer and spirituality that needs to be tapped into and made easily and widely available. We are and have always been a people of prayer. These spiritual resources are not just valuable for those within the Christian community but are worth making available to those who are seeking a spirituality within our broader society, who are possibly seeking God without quite knowing it.

Lift up your hearts

The prayer to which the first Christians – and we – are called to be faithful originated in Jewish prayer as we saw above, and there is a particular spirit and structure to such biblical prayer. It is based on the past which it recalls and gives thanks for and then it calls on God to continue to be present and at work among human beings. This spirit and structure is present in the Eucharistic Prayers of the Mass and so we will look at them in particular to see inside the nature of Christian prayer.

As the community of faith enters into the Eucharistic Prayer, the presiding priest invites them to lift up their hearts. As human beings, our hearts are tied up in many things especially in the cares of everyday life. This is part of our very nature as human beings. The above phrase invites us to raise our hearts beyond their constant preoccupations – not to leave them behind – but to take them into our relationship with God, to put them in the context of our relationship with God. It is an invitation to place ourselves in all situations in the hands of the Father in imitation of those final words of Jesus on the cross: 'Father, into your hands I commend my spirit'. In response to which, the Father opened a way before him.

Lifting up our hearts is to place ourselves in the presence of God and to recognise that we live in a world which comes to us from God, to recognise that God is the very source of our concrete and individual existence. In is in him that we 'live and move and have our being' (Acts 17:28).

Prayer for others

It is the recognition that we all live and move and have our being in God that makes sense of praying for each other. In our prayer for others, we are falling back on the reality that we are all united in God. That is, that each one of us is united with all others because of the living link we all have with the God who is the source of the existence of each one of us. We can, so to speak, commune with each other through our communing with the God who is giving life to all of us. We could perhaps put it this way: that we seek to join God in his giving life and grace to the person for whom we are praying.

The Lord be with you

Preceding the invitation to lift up our hearts, the presiding priest greets the gathered people with the words: 'The Lord be with you' and they reply, "And with your spirit'. This constantly repeated greeting throughout the Mass, recalls the reality that all that occurs within the liturgy is only possible because the Lord is already with us. It is the Lord who enables us to lift up our hearts. Any prayer arises in us because God has made the first move in us. This greeting takes the form of an expressed desire rather than a simple 'The Lord is with you' because we do have to turn to the Lord who is present with us, we do have to alert ourselves to his presence.

We give thanks, we intercede

Following the invitation to lift up our hearts comes the next invitation: "Let us give thanks to the Lord our God" and "It is right and just". The first movement of prayer is that of giving thanks for the constant life-giving relationship we have with God which has reached its high point in the gift of new life in Christ. We gave thanks for our very existence, for the world in which we live, for all the gifts that surround us. We acknowledge that we ourselves and our world are, in the first instance, God's gift.

The Eucharistic Prayer begins in thanksgiving and concludes in intercession. It is prayed in the awareness that the work of the creating and redeeming God has not yet reached its completion and so the whole celebration occurs in the spirit of creation's groaning for completion. We hold before God our entire struggling world as it is immersed in its own birth pangs as we also hold before God the needs that immediately surround us.

The Lord's Prayer

The Lord's Prayer is precious to us as the prayer handed down to us from the Lord through the gospels.

It begins with the word 'Father' which reflects Jesus' use of the affectionate word he used for his Father and ours, which is the Aramaic word 'Abba'. This immediately sets the tone for the whole prayer, giving it the flavour of closeness which is implied in the very use of that Aramaic word.

Without attempting a commentary on the Lord's Prayer, there are words and phrases within it which deserve at least a passing comment. Its first part is all about the Father: who dwells in heaven, who name is to be held holy, whose kingdom is to come, whose will is to be done on earth as in heaven.[65]

The Father is in heaven beyond the world as we know it even though he is so close to us that we can call him 'Abba'. We pray that the Father's holiness be recognised and proclaimed. It is in him that we truly find what is good. We pray that his kingdom may come, that is that his ways and his type of power might shape the world. We pray that his will be done on earth as in heaven, that is that his will be done willingly and gladly as it is in heaven.

The second part of the prayer is centred on the human beings praying the prayer: prayer for daily bread, for forgiveness of our debts and for the capacity to forgive our debtors, a prayer not to be put to the test, and a prayer to be saved from evil.

The deep humanity of the prayer comes out in this second section. It is basic prayer. It is prayer for our daily bread, that is

---

[65] For a detailed presentation of the Lord's Prayer, see Gerhard Lohfink, *The Our Father*, Collegeville, Minnesota: Liturgical Press, 2019.

for what keeps us going day by day which is so basic a need. It is striking that the prayer for forgiveness is cast in terms of the abolition of debts, that is the cancellation of our debts (sins). To pray that our debts be absolved is quite radical – we pray not just for their alleviation but their cancellation, their being set aside! And the prayer to be able to forgive the debts owed to us is really a prayer for the expansion of our hearts in order to be able to do it.

The prayer not to be put to the test is again the prayer of human beings who know themselves, who know that they may not manage to overcome the test.[66] And the prayer to be delivered from evil shows again the awareness of human weakness praying not to have to face the evil which has power in our world and can be so destructive.

★★★

There have been countless writings on prayer. Their variety illustrates the rich and multifaceted character of human relationships with God. The above chapter only touches the surface of all that could be said but it is enough to satisfy the purposes of this book.

---

[66] 'Test' is the better translation of the Greek word than is 'temptation'

CONCLUSION

We do not know what the future holds as we move on into it. But we do know from our knowledge of the past that new times, new ideas, new movements have constantly arisen and have been formative of the times following them. And so we seek to discern and respond to such things in our own times.

Whether we like it or not, our world is changing and the Church is changing along with it and within it. Changes in the Church happen sometimes as part of the changes in the world of which it is part and sometimes because of re-discoveries of the Church's own tradition and identity.

We cannot afford to pretend that all is as it has ever been. Despite the strong continuity that is clearly part of the Christian Tradition, there are also constant elements of discontinuity in the history of that tradition at the existential, pastoral, doctrinal, ethical and practical levels. We cannot presume that the faith as it has been handed on to us by those who have immediately gone before us, is exactly as it has been from the beginning. And we cannot project the particular form of the faith we have experienced back onto the whole of the Church's history. We need to look at our history and tradition concretely and accurately.

As mentioned in the Introduction to this book, we cannot let fear or timidity shape our present attitudes or our movement into the Church's future. That would be fatal humanly speaking and would be especially so for a People who believe in the unending fidelity of the good God, who raised Jesus the Christ out of death into life, beyond all expectations. That same God is still at work among us.

Conclusion

As Christians, anything which ever remotely hints of death must turn our minds to passing over into a new life. We believe in the One who continues to make the world out of nothing and who continues to give life to those who die, and who continues to open a way ahead for his people. Is a Christian without that sure and certain hope really a Christian?

We are in a situation parallel to that of Abraham our father in faith. In response to God's call, he made a break with what went before him even though it was that which had formed and nurtured him. But his response to that call to move on produced a new and renewing opening into the future.

And so for Catholic Christians today! We have inherited a long and enriching tradition which has gone through many historical phases and modifications. Now, at this time, we are called to produce a new growth in that tradition, a new branch that will flourish in the future. We, like Abraham our father in faith, are being called into a future that God "will show us".

Appendix
A MODEL FOR THE FUTURE

The Rite of Christian Initiation for Adults

The *Rite of the Christian Initiation of Adults* (whose Latin version was published in 1972 and whose English version was published in 1987) has been used in many parishes throughout the Catholic world in initiating adults into the Christian faith. Parallel forms of it have been used in the initiation of school aged children (RCIC). The rites outlined in this process are the hinges of the whole process which itself goes well beyond them.

Most of the process of this initiation involves meeting in groups with discussions, the sharing of experiences, explanatory input and prayer. The rituals which are part of the process are the means of moving from one stage of the process to another. The whole process is intentionally very flexible. A group of people from the parish or its equivalent accompany those interested in becoming Catholic.

In the process outlined in the RCIA – often referred to as the Catechumenate – we can see a model for the Church's general evangelisation in the new societal context in which it finds itself. There are four stages of the process of initiation outlined in the document. The first stage is that of Inquiry which, as its name suggests, is based on discovering the prompts which have led the person to be interested in the gospel and the Church and so by extension discovering something of their personal life journey, along with their questions and their difficulties. This stage seeks to encourage an initial encounter of the enquirers with Christ and his gospel.

There then follows the period of the Catechumenate during which there is reflection over the Scriptures, explanation of the gospel and the tradition of the Church along with time for prayer.

The third period is the time of Lent which concentrates upon the Paschal Mystery to be celebrated at Easter at which feast those preparing are initiated by baptism, confirmation and first communion in the Eucharist.

Any people who have already been baptised in another Christian tradition are confirmed and receive their first Communion in the Catholic Church. This period also emphasises the spiritual preparation of those to be initiated.

The fourth period follows initiation at the Easter Vigil. In this period, the newly initiated reflect on their experience and have Christian faith presented to them more thoroughly and at greater depth.

This process of initiation provides a model for the Church's evangelising activity. It respects and takes seriously the background and present situation of those with some interest in the gospel and seeks to draw together the person's concrete situation and the gospel as a response to their seeking for meaning and fulfilment in their lives.

It presents the gospel and the Christian tradition quite thoroughly but always in response to the experience of those interested. It surrounds those interested with a group of people through whom they begin to experience the life of the Church.

The same process of initiation offers a serious presentation of the Christian faith. It stretches over a considerable period of time during which the bases of Catholic Christianity are presented and the meaning and purpose of human life is outlined as it is seen in the light of believing in Christ. Those taking part in this introduction into the Christian life are introduced to prayer and to the Eucharist and the other sacraments which are constitutive of being a Catholic Christian. It makes clear that the Christian life journey is indeed a journey which is not just that of an individual but one that is undertaken in the company of and with the support of other believers.

www.ingramcontent.com/pod-product-compliance
Lightning Source LLC
Chambersburg PA
CBHW012005090526
44590CB00026B/3882